Stock Detective
Investor

Stock Detective Investor

Finding Market Gems Online

Kevin Lichtman
Lynn N. Duke

John Wiley & Sons, Inc.

New York • Chichester • Weinheim • Brisbane • Singapore • Toronto

Published by John Wiley & Sons, Inc.
Published simultaneously in Canada.

This publication is designed to provide accurate and authoritative information in regard to the subject matter covered. It is sold with the understanding that the publisher is not engaged in rendering professional services. If professional advice or other expert assistance is required, the services of a competent professional person should be sought.

Library of Congress Cataloging-in-Publication Data:

Lichtman, Kevin, 1960–
    Stock detective investor : finding market gems online / Kevin Lichtman and Lynn N. Duke.
       p.   cm.
    Includes index.
    ISBN 0-471-38775-4 (cloth : alk. paper)
    1. Investments—Computer network resources. 2. Electronic trading of securities. 3. Stocks—Computer network resources. I. Duke, Lynn, 1959–   II. Title.
HG4515.95 .L53 2001
332.63'22'02854678—dc21

00-043740

10 9 8 7 6 5 4 3 2 1

In loving memory of
Sidney and Dorothy Lichtman

K.L.

To my parents,
Gaeton and Vilma Nucci,
for teaching me that anything is possible,
and to my husband,
Glen Duke,
for proving that it's true

L.N.D.

FOREWORD

E very investor dreams of owning shares of the next
Microsoft, Cisco System, or America Online. Unscrupulous stock promoters and brokers prey on this desire with
pie-in-the-sky pitches for low-priced stocks boasting the latest "revolutionary" product or technology. Too often, there's
neither product nor technology—and no revenues and no
future.

In fact, a company's insiders may seek only to pump up
the stock price and dump the shares at a big profit—for them.
Promoters shrewdly use Internet, e-mail, or direct mail to target unknowing investors. This form of fraud and deceit is
growing. The Securities and Exchange Commission estimates
annual investor losses to penny-stock fraud at $6 billion.

Stock Detective Investor boldly takes on the schemes, scams,
and scums that lurk in the little-known, little-examined dark,
grimy netherworld of investing.

Kevin Lichtman launched the original Stock Detective as
part of the FinancialWeb.com Web site in the summer of 1997
(www.stockdetective.com). As a stock promoter turned re-
former, Kevin could smell a rat but he had no experience or

training in the rigors of investigative journalism. Award-winning news reporter Lynn Duke, a fighter for the individual investor, joined the venture that fall. Together, they pursued and exposed fishy stock promotions and companies that made inflated claims. Indeed, Stock Detective achieved an impressive track record in busting "pump 'n' dump" schemes and other market shenanigans.

The work of Kevin and Lynn did not go unnoticed. Chicago *Sun-Times* financial columnist Terry Savage, for example, lauded Stock Detective in her June 6, 1999, column, stating: "I'd rank this Web site as the greatest advance in investor protection since the SEC was created half a century ago." *Stock Detective Investor* strives to live up to such lofty praise.

Investors who dare tread into the choppy waters of penny stocks should know what they're up against. *Stock Detective Investor* helps chart a steady course for these investors and highlights the resources available to protect them. You'll need this book's do-it-yourself approach to investor protection, because the Securities and Exchange Commission is short on staff and funds to sufficiently combat the growth of securities fraud.

If you like David Letterman's "top 10" lists, you'll benefit from this book's list of 10 warning signs of possible stock fraud. When should an investor exercise a health skepticism about a company?

Stock Detective Investor also provides understandable explanations of complicated subjects such as reverse mergers, Regulation D, and "scalping"—and how these vehicles are used by unscrupulous stock promoters. There's useful commentary on investing via the Internet, including tips for online traders and warnings about online message boards. And there's a comprehensive list of names, street addresses, telephone and fax numbers, and e-mail addresses for securities regulators in all 50 states, the District of Columbia, and all Canadian provinces.

But the strongest asset of this book is the passion of its authors. Kevin and Lynn firmly believe in their cause because of the letters they receive from real people like "Jason" who was scammed out of thousands of dollars. Although more eloquently written than most, Jason's letter spoke for many novices lured by the potential of Internet-induced investment riches. Here are some portions from the actual letter:

> I bought shares of [XYZ Corp.] and [ABCD Inc.] after hearing about them from [a Web site] . . . I made rash decisions based solely upon the advice I was getting from one source over the Internet, but I kept rationalizing my actions. I saw how trading volume went way up when "a newsletter" profiled a stock, so I thought they had to be for real. I watched ABCD gain nearly 50 percent in just a few weeks, only to fall shortly thereafter . . .
>
> I thought they were doing me a favor by giving me these hot leads over the Internet, before word of them circulated into the general populace. Then I watched both XYZ and ABCD move steadily downward, but I convinced myself this was just a temporary setback. I saw [OKOK Corp.] moving up, and decided to buy some of that, too. It had only been three or four months since I started investing in the newsletter's monthly picks, and I was brimming with optimism . . .

Then the bottom fell out of OKOK so quickly, I didn't know what hit me . . . Both XYZ and ABCD are worth substantially less than when I bought them. I think I got as burned as anyone could get on OKOK, buying at 12⅞ per share. I don't have to tell you what it's worth now . . .

Don't be another Jason, Don't let this happen to you.

CARL SURRAN
Editor, FinancialWeb.com

ACKNOWLEDGMENTS

I've long believed that an important part of a successful investor is his or her skill at not losing money. In 1997, I began publishing the Stock Detective Internet site supposing visitors would benefit from a journal that exposed potential stock scams and taught investors how to avoid losses.

In the earliest days, Jeff Grossman, FinancialWeb's small-cap editor, helped me spot potential stock scams to report. Then, I somehow persuaded Carl Surran to come work for me. Eventually, Carl hoodwinked Lynn Duke into leaving a respectable job to pursue Wall Street perpetrators for us. Together, we made a great team and exposed dozens of online stock scandals and swindles long before most of our more well-known colleagues in the financial media.

Along the way, Stock Detective got noticed. *Smart Money* said we were "a site for underachieving investments and a support group for those who think they've been duped." *Worth* magazine declared, "Stock Detective has an enviable track record for fingering overhyped stocks." *Forbes* urged its readers to check us out.

Yes. We received hate mail too. But more important, there were hundreds of e-mails from investors thanking us for shining a light their way or urging us to investigate a lead. I wish I had saved all of those, but I will never forget the one that simply began: "Thank you, thank you, thank you."

Gayle Essary, whom I believe was the real "Waco Kid," deserves credit for turning me on to the Internet. I'd like to thank Om Malik, from *Forbes*, for his perpetual enthusiasm for our work. Kudos go to Mark Beauchamp, of the North American Securities Administrators Association, for inviting me to speak in front of all those intimidating faces. And, thanks to columnist and author, Terry Savage, who paid the single most impressive compliment Stock Detective ever received and then urged Debby Englander of John Wiley & Sons to consider publishing a "Stock Detective" book.

Finally, thanks to my family and friends for their patience, understanding, and support.

KEVIN LICHTMAN

This book is not only the result of months of reporting and writing, it's the culmination of several years' work during which I came in contact with hundreds of people who unselfishly shared their knowledge, and sometimes their embarrassments, in the hope of helping others become better investors. To all of you who helped make Stock Detective a success online, many thanks.

More specifically, I thank John Reed Stark at the U.S. Securities and Exchange Commission for his time and effort, and John Heine in the Commission's press office for assistance in gathering information. Other organizations that were invaluable in researching this book include The National Association of Securities Dealers, particularly the regulatory department; the North American Securities Administrators Association; and the California Department of Corporations.

I also thank the current management at FinancialWeb .com, especially Editor-in-Chief Carl Surran, for their continued commitment to investor education.

Michael Roban was instrumental in getting this project launched, and Debra Englander at John Wiley & Sons singlehandedly oversaw its completion. Many other people helped in the writing of this book, although most may not realize it. Family and friends lent unwavering support throughout the most difficult and tedious times. You know who you are. Thanks!

LYNN N. DUKE

CONTENTS

INTRODUCTION

The wild ride of the 1980s, coupled with the rise of the Internet, has put many investors in an envious yet precarious position. The large number of investment opportunities has led to burgeoning portfolios, and new technology allows quick access to more information than most people ever knew existed. And yet, securities fraud escalated almost as rapidly as the Dow in the latter half of the 1990s. The Securities and Exchange Commission (SEC) finally assigned a fraud division to the specific task of combating Internet crimes.

So, where's the downside to a rising market, better policing by the government, and an informed public?

The bull market of the 1990s allowed many otherwise prudent people to go a little wild. They invested in companies they never would have glanced at before. Meanwhile, the Internet gave a whole new cadre of scam artists cheap entry into investors' radar screens. Even with its special focus on Internet scams, the SEC is likely to have difficulty keeping up with the growing number of frauds.

What does the easy access to information mean for the new breed of savvy investors? It has been virtually untapped.

The baby boomers didn't give up on instant gratification when they logged on and started investing. If anything, the market's recent spectacular run has only fueled the craving.

However, people are starting to pay more attention. Some have been scammed, some have a nagging feeling that they're about to be scammed, and some are just plain smart. Since 1997, StockDetective.com has been a resource for people who want to mine the Internet for investment opportunities while cutting through all the babble and hype. In this book, we'll show how we research and report on new companies and so-called "hot" investments.

Even if (unlike us) you don't go looking for scams, they are bound to find you. If a proposal sounds too good to be true, it probably is. If you don't believe that, keep reading. This book spells out what all the fine print in prospectuses *really* means.

From the essentials of a Form 10-K to the technique for peeling off the layers of paid promotion, this book will focus on step-by-step analysis. You'll learn:

- When you should worry if revenue has been booked as a receivable. (When there's no guarantee it will be received.)
- The difference between weighted and diluted shares, and why you should care about it. (Determining fully diluted shares gives you a more accurate accounting of what your own holdings are actually worth.)

We won't just walk you through final reports, SEC filings, and those slick glossy annual reports. We'll show you how to take your online research a step further. By using

Web sites, stock screens, and search engines, you can convert hours of wading through gibberish into a breezy afternoon of surfing.

We hope that, by reading this book and referring to it before you make new investments, you'll not only become a smarter investor who can spot and avoid scams, but you'll understand that, amid all the boring details, there are clues that will enable you to make smart investment decisions.

Stock Detective
Investor

1

DÉJÀ VU—A HISTORY OF STOCK SCAMS

"I have always thought that if in the lamentable era of the 'New Economics,' culminating in 1929, even in the presence of dizzily spiraling prices, we had all continuously repeated 'Two and two still make four,' much of the evil might have been averted."

Bernard Baruch

Stock fraud, which now runs rampant on the Internet, may have found a new medium, but charlatans pushing penny stocks are nothing new to the investment community. Today's scams, moving at cyber speed, evolved from the high-pressured telemarketing ruses of the early 1980s. That's when cold calling for sales—practiced mainly west of the Mississippi and targeted toward people who were generally more isolated from financial centers and less sophisticated about the ways of Wall Street—invaded major metropolitan areas and the population-rich East Coast.

Prior to that invasion, stock fraud had quite a run in the middle of the twentieth century, when cheap gold and silver mining stocks were heaped on unsuspecting investors who were newly flush with post-World War II riches.

Going back still further, to the early 1900s, Charles Ponzi foisted on investors the first *pyramid scheme* (the money from later contributors is used to pay off early investors). Scams based on this pattern would eventually bear Ponzi's name.

Ponzi schemes have enjoyed a renaissance in recent years; the schemers use the Internet to reach a wider pool of victims. But today's pyramid schemes have a twist that most often relieves investors of their money. "Pump 'n' dump" scams amplify the pyramid hoax: Investors funneling into the market on the pump inevitably bankroll huge profits for those who got in earlier. The difference here is that, more than likely, the earliest investors know what is going on. In a Ponzi scheme, everyone's flying blind. The vehicle of choice for this feat of economic engineering is typically a thinly traded penny stock.

During the 1980s, the number of brokerage firms specializing in penny stocks increased more than fivefold. From beginnings in only five states, they expanded their base of operations to 25 states.

And why not? In less than 20 years, the number of households that held securities went from one-in-seventeen in 1980 to one-in-three by 1997, according to the North American Securities Administrators Association.

The Securities and Exchange Commission (SEC) estimates investors' losses to penny stock fraud at $6 billion annually (triple what it was in 1980) and still growing. Yet the SEC's resources to fight fraud—both online and via traditional telemarketing—have not kept pace. The odds of getting caught keep going down.

During the recent bull market, U.S. investors have been raking in billions on everything from blue chips to start-ups. But thousands of people funneled their funds into stock scams, many of which were launched on the Internet.

Once the exclusive domain of cold-callers telephoning from boiler rooms around the country, stock market fraud has cast its own Web around the world. The Internet has made it vastly more affordable, and much simpler, to trick an unsuspecting public.

The medium may have changed, but the message has not. Easy money is out there, but only the savviest investors need apply. In this age of political correctness and sensitivity, even charlatans are beginning to turn their backs on the high-pressure scare tactics that used to come steaming out of the boiler rooms. Instead, they appeal to ego and wit.

Stock Detective is dedicated to educating investors, not only about how to spot a scam, but how to intelligently mine the Internet for investment opportunities.

The simplest advice for investors is: Follow a common-sense rule. If something sounds too good to be true, it probably is. But to err is human, so here are the major warning signs investors should keep in mind when the urge to get rich quick from a flaky idea becomes overwhelming.

Cheaper, Better, Faster: Spam and Other Delicacies

In windowless rooms, littered with takeout castoffs and coffee cups, and lathered in smoke and stale sweat, the predators flex and preen. At one time, they wiggled an index finger before dialing a cold call. Now, that same digit reaches thousands of potential victims in a single keystroke.

Back in the days of phone-based stock scams, a boiler room full of phone jockeys might be lucky to reach several thousand potential victims on any given day. The Internet is rapidly increasing the odds of hitting pay dirt.

There are two types of promoters. The first type, the pure public relations (PR) people, have been paid by the company, or by someone with an interest in the company, to hype the stock in hopes that the price will spike while certain people are poised to sell. These promoters in particular have moved to the Internet, where talk is cheap and the available eyeballs increase exponentially on a daily basis.

But another group often stands to make as much money as the promoters, and sometimes as much as company insiders. Most investors never see or hear about this second group. They are the broker-dealers who get huge chunks of shares—usually at a deep discount—and turn around and sell the shares through the front door at enormous profit. The fictionalized chop shop of J.T. Marlin, depicted in the film *Boiler Room*, wasn't too far from the truth. The snazzy cars, the shameless browbeating of hapless investors, and, ultimately, the arrests made by the feds are common realities.

When Is a Promotion a Scam?

When the SEC busted dozens of stock promoters in October 1998, it was the agency's first nationwide sweep in the Internet Age. But it wasn't the first time the government had focused on penny stocks. As surely as bull markets attract lots of money, they also seem to inspire the morally challenged. During the great market run in the 1980s, penny stock fraud grew so rampant that an SEC task force called for several changes.

Among them were stricter guidelines for brokers to follow to ensure investor suitability, and approval of a pilot project by the National Association of Securities Dealers (NASD) that launched the electronic bulletin board. Many thought that when information on thinly traded micro-cap stocks became available electronically, it would trip up the scam artists. But the advent of another electronic medium, the Internet, and a fresh bull market in the mid-1990s, simply fed them fresh fuel.

The 1998 crackdown, and the others that have followed, did not do much to deter the spinmeisters from deceiving the public. However, many hype artists have gone to charm school. Instead of completely ignoring the SEC's rules pertaining to paid promotion, they have moved toward ambiguity or a simple game of hide-and-seek.

The SEC requires that anyone who has been paid to promote a stock must disclose who paid, how much, and in what form (cash or stock). The rules also require a promoter's disclosure of any position in a stock (even if those shares were not compensation from the company for services). Finally, the government prohibits promoters from encouraging investors to buy shares in one breath, while selling their own in the next. This is called scalping, and the SEC has been savage about pursuing these infractions.

In light of these rules, and in the wake of the SEC's sweeps, many promoters have feigned compliance with the rule. But don't be fooled. A disclaimer that says "We have a position in Company X and may buy or sell in that position at any time" is simply telling investors that the promoters might or might not scalp their shares. Disclaimers stating that the company may or may not be compensated, or that it has been compensated but the form or denomination is not revealed, are also shams.

Even promoters who comply with the SEC rules usually make the information difficult for investors to ferret out. Links within links, wild-goose-chase links, and fine print that would make a jeweler go blind put most disclaimers in the "not worth my while" category in the Internet's realm of instant gratification. And promoters are counting on a short attention span—one of the hallmarks of the generations weaned first on television, then on video games, and now online.

Pretty in Pink

Stocks that didn't meet the minimum listing requirements for Nasdaq (National Association of Securities Dealers Automated Quotations System) climbed out of the "pink sheets" and onto the electronic over-the-counter bulletin board in the 1990s. The pink sheets, a daily publication that many brokers subscribed to, offered the only way to get quotes on stocks that weren't listed on any organized exchange. In 1990, the bulletin board was established.

For most of the decade, the bulletin board—like the pink sheets before it—was a great hiding place for companies that wanted to avoid the SEC's radar. Until 1999, the only filing requirements were those required by the state in which the company was incorporated.

During a 19-month period that began in January 1999, stocks traded on the bulletin board had to start filing with the SEC. This presented problems to companies, whether they were legit or a little shady, because an SEC filing is neither a laughing nor an inexpensive matter.

What were companies doing before their attention was turned toward the business of an SEC filing?

One Louisiana-based firm managed to squeeze $24,000 from investors before being shut down. Its premise: It was going to "build,"—yes, *build*—a new island in the Caribbean Sea. Ten 300′ × 300′ platforms were planned for this New Utopia. That's roughly the size of a large mall but perfect for the financial world's next Dodge City, and the term "off shore" gained a new twist.

New Utopia's self-proclaimed Prince consented to a judgment that included an order that he not violate a host of SEC rules, and that ordered him to pay back the $24,000. However, according to an SEC Litigation Release, the same order waived this payment based on his "sworn showing of inability to pay. Moreover, the Court did not order . . . to pay a civil penalty because of his demonstrated inability to pay." More on crime and punishment later.

And just because a company starts reporting to the SEC, investors should not let down their guard. Many companies continue attracting attention to themselves with dubious claims and startling predictions that should put any investor on edge.

Here are a couple of examples of spam that crossed the North American Securities Administrators Association

---

BIO-TECH BREAKTHROUGH!!

Company: Endovasc Ltd. Inc.
Symbol: ENDV
Price: ½ ($0.50/share)

The April issue of the British Biotechnology Letter, Oxford, England, states: "Scientists at Glaxo Wellcome have proven the efficacy of Endovasc's PGE-1 and have submitted to management a multimillion-dollar joint venture proposal."

ENDV is recommended as an immediate and "STRONG BUY."

URGENT BUY ALERT!!

Company: PDC Innovative Industries
Symbol: PDCID
Price: 5 ($5/share)

PDCID has announced priority production of their proprietary Hypo-Sterile 2000, which renders medical contaminants harmless. Analysts indicate there is "almost limitless demand in the marketplace for this revolutionary stand-alone medical device."

PDCID is rated an immediate and "STRONG BUY"

(NASAA) desk that the organization said were "typical examples of 'spams' to thousands of other unsuspecting investors" sent by broker/dealers without the authorization or even knowledge of the subject company.

Endovasc Ltd. is still a going concern, and its president refuted the press release when it came out, disclaiming any knowledge of its source. PDC Innovative Industries is no longer in business.

This might all sound interesting to a novice, but anyone with a shred of investing savvy would want to know:

1. Where's the documentation to back up the claims?
2. Who's making all the noise?
3. What's in it for the noisemakers?

Even seemingly innocuous statements should be cause for concern. One of the most common, and plausibly benign, is the tendency to describe themselves as Nasdaq-listed when in fact they don't qualify for that exchange.

Perhaps the confusion lies in the parent regulator of the Nasdaq and the over-the-counter bulletin board (OTCBB): the National Association of Securities Dealers (NASD).

The Nasdaq (National Association of Securities Dealers Automated Quotations System) consists of two tiers: (1) small cap and (2) national market. Companies must meet specific criteria, including market capitalization, minimum bid/ask, and net tangible assets. (See Appendix D for listing requirements).

The OTCBB, which was established and is maintained by the NASD, had virtually no criteria (other than demand) for carrying a quote. The SEC began phasing in filing requirements in 1999.

Those requirements were based on three rules first proposed by the NASD in 1998:

http://www.otcbb.com/news/EligibilityRule/nasdboardmtg.stm

1. OTC Bulletin Board Eligibility Rule—Permit only those domestic companies that report their current financial information to the SEC, banking, or insurance regulators to be quoted on the OTCBB. If an issuer is delinquent in its reports, there will be a grace period of 30 days during which Market Makers may continue to quote the security. Nonreporting companies whose securities are already quoted on the OTCBB will have 6–12 months to comply with the new requirements once the rule becomes effective.

2. Recommendation Rule—Require brokerage firms to review current financial statements (i.e., put out in the last 12 months) about the issuer before they recommend a transaction in any OTC security (a security that is not listed on Nasdaq—or any registered national securities exchange). Additionally, firms must designate a qualified registered individual to review the information required by the rule.

3. Disclosure Rule—Require brokerage firms to provide investors with written disclosure of the differences between OTC securities and those that trade on a listed market. The disclosure statement will be provided on each customer's confirmation following any trade in an OTC security.

Companies that fail to file get bumped from the electronic bulletin board and must go back to the pink sheets, where they all wallowed just a decade ago. But there are even some rumblings that the pink sheets might go online, although under whose regulation or watchful eye, it's not clear. And even if filing requirements have tamed the most outrageous claims, they have also turned ambiguity into art.

Weak Fundamentals

The Internet has changed the rules on Wall Street in several ways. First, the dot-coms, such as Amazon, eBay, and Yahoo!, defy almost every piece of practical logic and analysis by which a company's value has been judged historically. Hundreds of millions of dollars in the hole? Investors will bid it up higher and faster than brokers in a chop shop.

Second, the sheer volume of new investors who have access to desktop trading has changed the dynamics of the market. According to a SEC report issued in November 1999, http://www.sec.gov/news/studies/cybexsum.htm, the number of online brokerage accounts topped 9.7 million in the second quarter of 1999, up from 3.7 million accounts less than two years earlier.

A state securities regulator recently recalled how Wall Street legend Bernard Baruch bailed out of the bull market in 1929, just weeks before its fatal crash. While in an airport, the regulator overheard two older women swapping stock tips. One had bought heavily into a dot-com start-up, based on a tip from the receptionist at her beauty parlor. The regulator quipped that, if he were to follow Baruch's example, it was time to get out of the market. Baruch, the story goes, sold his holdings—and avoided much of the market's wrath—after receiving a tip from a shoeshine boy. But even this is fiction. In his biography of Baruch, James Grant says that Baruch "did not buy the market at the 1932 bottom any more than he sold it at the 1929 top."

The Internet has changed the rules and has given more investors access to more information than some professionals had just a short time ago. But it hasn't given them a formal education.

Most investors don't know the difference between a balance sheet and a spreadsheet, although P/E ratios are now cocktail chatter. But dot-coms are sexy, and one of them has got to be the next Microsoft, so the dot-com market has been run up to a trillion-dollar market capitalization, even though the companies—combined—have sales of only about $50 billion and, taken as a group, are in the red.

"There's a huge market value based on the expectation, hype, and hope that the Internet is the economy of the future," said Bill McDonald, enforcement director for the California Department of Corporations. "Silly old-fashioned things like profits are not the indicators of success."

Something for Nothing?

Now that the SEC requires all companies trading on the over-the-counter bulletin board to start filing, it's a snap to find out how much key players at a company are paid. Certain employees, and all directors, must disclose all forms of compensation—salaries, deferred pay, stock, options, company cars, housing, and other perks. But don't expect to find this information highlighted at the top of the report. You've got to look for it. (A simple keyword search will move things along.) But it's worth checking to see how well company executives are paying themselves. Then ask whether the compensation packages are in line with the rest of the company's financial state, and whether the person cashing the checks has the credentials to justify them.

The SEC requires another tidbit, usually in a proxy statement: Who's related to whom within a company? Is the company doing business with relatives? There's nothing wrong with this connection on its face. But tracing a web of relationships can sometimes clarify a decision about whether a company's funds are in the right place.

Suspicious Backgrounds

While you're perusing those SEC documents for salaries and nepotism, read up on the backgrounds of the officers and directors. A former insurance salesman is now running an Internet software company? A businessperson under investigation by the feds has been named president of a firm involved in technology research—halfway across the country? Many U.S. corporations have been built from scratch by men and women whose credentials might seem to lead elsewhere, but none of them was pandering for your start-up capital, either.

Again, this is where a little digging—especially in the proxy statement—can pay off. Is the board stacked with the founder's relatives and business associates? Is that their only qualification for helping to steer the company?

Involvement in Unrelated Businesses

Just as you want a company's officers and directors well grounded in the business at hand, the company should be focused, also. When a contractor gets involved in medical research, take a second look. If a sportswear company starts selling frozen yogurt, make sure you see the financials before buying a single share.

Reverse Splits

Reverse splits are suspect because they often are simply smoke and mirrors, or a ploy setting the stage for a secondary offering.

Most investors are familiar with splits. Many salivate for them, especially among hot issues on a meteoric rise. A forward split cuts the stock price by whatever ratio is used; the theory is that it will be more affordable to a wider range of investors at the lower price. For example, a two-for-one stock split would halve the share price, and a three-for-one split would cut the price by two-thirds. At the time of the split, shareholders have more shares but their *total* value is the same as before the split. (Ten shares at $100 apiece become 20 shares at $50 each. Either way, it's $1,000 worth of stock.) But if the stock price continues rising, then investors of record before the split have twice as much stock increasing in value.

In contrast, a reverse split increases the share price based on whatever factor the company chooses. For example, 100 shares of stock trading at $1 apiece, after a 1-for-10, or reverse split, would become 10 shares valued at $10 apiece. Often, a reverse split is engineered based on the idea that "more is more." Investors might not even glance at a stock trading below $5 (beware the penny stock rules!). But it's more likely to hit their radar if the price is higher, even if it's artificially inflated.

The first questions investors should ask are: Why doesn't this company's stock price rise on its own? Why does it need the help of a reverse split? Another warning sign after a reverse split: A company makes a secondary offering based on the new (higher) share price. This allows it to raise more new capital with fewer shares, but it also quickly dilutes the holdings of investors who were in before the reverse split.

Irregularities Posing as Regulations and Other Sleights of Hand

Before shares of stock are traded on the open market, they must either be registered with the SEC or qualify for exemption from registration under SEC rules. Regulation D is one of those exemptions. Its sister, Regulation S, was a favorite of stock scammers (especially offshore operators) before a revised rule became effective in 1998 and all but eliminated it as a loophole. At that time, the SEC changed the holding period for Regulation-S-issued securities from 40 days to one year. Other restrictions were added in a further effort to deter fraud. When the one-year holding period expires, the shares are still restricted under Rule 144, or another exemption. These rules apply only to U.S. corporations.

Regulation D of the Securities Act of 1933 lays out the rules for offering and selling unregistered stock. Plenty of companies use this as a legitimate way to raise money, usually by selling to qualified investors. But it's not a carte blanche to issue stock. Regulation D restricts the amount of money that can be raised, limits how many people can share in the offering, and sometimes stipulates the type of investor who can buy in. http://www.law.uc.edu/CCL/33ActRls/regD.html

So why is this a warning sign? Unregistered securities, despite SEC scrutiny, can still be used to turn worthless paper into cash. These shares can be issued for next to nothing. Once they become available for free trading (often timed to align with a promotion or other pump in the market), the investors dump the shares, which they got for pennies, for $1, $3—and sometimes $20 or $30. They take away an enormous profit, dilute the shares that others bought at inflated prices, and then disappear when the stock is at a 52-week high and has no place to go but down.

Convertibles are another stealth weapon against naïve investors. Companies may clearly state how many convertibles have been issued, and their terms. But investors who are not paying attention could buy into a company whose stock could become grossly diluted with just a few transactions. Always do the math.

Quirks and Crannies

There are other indicators that sometimes also mean trouble.

Late filings with the SEC could signal a problem in the accounting department. An occasional late filing is not uncommon; in fact, it happens in most companies. But if a thinly traded, overhyped stock can't get its books in order, on time, two or three quarters in a row, then you might want to chat with the CFO—if there is one.

Similarly, if a company is always in court, investors might want to scrutinize its activities and how it deals with litigation. Is it facing several class action suits from angry investors or consumers? What is the potential for damages, and what is the company's defense?

Also take a look at the company's trading history and, for many Nasdaq and bulletin board stocks, the market makers.

Market makers, as the name implies, create a market for a stock by maintaining solid bid and ask prices for the shares, and are committed to buying round lots at publicly quoted prices. Nothing wrong with this, on its face, but do you know who the market makers are? Most will be reputable firms going about their business. But if the name sounds familiar, but doesn't quite fit (*Boiler Room*'s J.T. Marlin is deceptively close to J.P. Morgan and is typical of attempts to gain credibility by association), dig deeper. Most stocks that have market makers have several, all of which can be found at the Over-the-Counter Bulletin Board site, http://www.otcbb .com/dynamic/. If none of the market makers' names rings a bell, dig deeper.

Finally, come back to a company's press releases. Volume and predictions aside, follow them like a thread tracing a company's story over time. Has a firm that was positioning itself in May as a software developer reinvented itself by October and created a business plan for telephone service in a former Russian republic?

A company that started out claiming it would be one of the Internet's first advertising giants devolved into an empty shell. It went through a series of mergers, reverse splits, and mission restatements, all swaddled in an endless stream of promotional hype and press releases. Meanwhile, many of the original players disappeared—perhaps into another empty shell.

2

BE YOUR OWN
STOCK DETECTIVE

*A Detailed, Step-by-Step Explanation
of How to Sort Out the Numbers*

It's no secret: Americans hate math. Numbers make us cringe, and we'll often feign a migraine rather than admit to our fourth graders that we don't know the actual formula for dividing fractions.

If you want to be a prudent investor, get over your fear of numbers.

For many people, the first time they look at a company's SEC filings, even if they manage to sift through all of the legal jargon, wading into the numbers leaves them shivering.

But with a few Stock Detective guidelines to get you through them quickly. Balance sheets, cash flow statements, and annual financial reports begin looking more like a travel brochure. Where do you want to go today? Surfing for some cheap shares in the tech industry's next big bang?

Before you go hunting for good investments, you have to define your investment goals. For most people, those goals are defined by balancing risk tolerance with time, capital, and diversification.

Okay, the ultimate goal is to be rich. Middle America has watched, dumfounded, in the past five years while seemingly everyone's net worth has climbed into seven figures and beyond.

Your neighbor bought stock in AOL back when all callers could get were busy signals. Now he drives a Porsche. Your cousin, the customer-service-clerk-for-life at Schwab is retiring as a millionaire employee because of her stock options. Television commercials for online brokerages feature truck drivers buying private islands, and soccer moms piling up money in portfolios, all by themselves.

Why not?

Get a computer, log on to the Internet, and pursue your piece of the American Dream. You probably already know someone who has.

Online investing has suddenly made it easy and affordable for consumers from all walks of life to invest in the stock market. With low transaction fees and instant access to a wealth of financial information, plus trading tools once reserved for the pros, small investors can pursue their own Warren Buffett-like goals.

Whoa. Not so fast.

Professional investors—people who pull a paycheck for investing other people's money—still have an advantage over mere pedestrians. Their 50-plus-hours workweek often spills over into leisure time as these folks keep digging for the winner that will "make" them. Nearly all have passed one or more securities licensing examinations.

Stock Detective gives individual investors the knowledge needed to perform some of the same analyses that the pros do. We'll show you what to look for and where to find it—hidden or otherwise.

But first, a review of the basics.

Of Risk and Reward

You've probably heard this before, but it's worth repeating: There is a very predictable relationship between risk and reward: The greater the risk, the greater the potential reward.

Don't like taking much risk? Fine. Stick with conservative, relatively low-interest-bearing investments like Treasury bonds or bank certificates of deposit. But you'll have to put away a lot of money quite regularly, and for a long time, before you can sidle up to your first Porsche.

Do you have a little broader time line, or a penchant for risk? Okay. But before moving your entire 401(k) to the newest dot-com barnstormer, let's review the elements of managing risk.

The key element in managing risk is asset allocation, or determining how to divvy up your assets among different classes of investments. Typically, investments are divided into three categories: cash, bonds, and stocks (in their ascending order of risk).

At the heart of allocation is *diversification*. Make sure your assets are divided in such a way that a single market event doesn't threaten your entire nest egg. But before you invest in anything, cash must be addressed.

Let's face it: Unless you're a reckless gambler, your first act of fiscal responsibility is to have at least enough cash on hand to pay all your living expenses for six months, even if you had no other form of income.

One element in managing risk and determining asset allocation is age. The closer you are to retirement, the fewer work years are left for replacing any investment losses.

Bonds really refer to all forms of time savings and fixed-income investments. These investments pay interest and promise to return a principal amount at the end of a specified term, usually one year or longer. Corporate and government bonds, and bank CDs are in this category. Bonds are considered a conservative investment, although they are riskier than cash. Their returns are spelled out at the time of issue.

Stocks, in general, are riskier than bonds. As you get older, a greater portion of your assets should move from equities into bonds. The general rule is that age should be inversely proportionate to risk in a portfolio. Many other variables—including inheritance, pensions, Social Security, and other personal financial holdings—will all play a role in how you invest your money.

And, finally, there's the sleep test. If your investments keep you awake at night, it's time to reexamine your portfolio.

Wall Street, Here I Come!

When you're ready to begin investing in stocks and bonds, the best place to begin is with mutual funds. By their very nature, mutual funds offer reduced risk through diversification.

If you have only a modest sum to invest in the stock market—say, less than $10,000—it's going to be difficult, if not impossible, to diversify your portfolio sufficiently to hedge against the risk that one investment could destroy much of your wealth.

First, remember that mutual funds do not invest solely in stocks. There are more than 7,000 U.S. mutual funds to choose from.

One type of stock mutual fund that has risen in popularity in recent years is what is known as an "index fund." Index funds are mutual funds that invest in a portfolio of stocks that mirrors the group of stocks that comprise a popular stock index such as the Dow Joes Industrial Average or the Standard & Poor's (S&P) 500. Index funds' fees are among the lowest because little research, analysis, or management is involved.

Because mutual funds invest in a diversified portfolio of stocks and other securities, their day-to-day performance is generally much less volatile, compared to most individual stocks. That fact makes mutual funds even more attractive for your longer-term investment strategies. Additionally, because most mutual funds allow you to make small periodic investments, they are very attractive for regular savings and for dollar cost-averaging investment strategies.

Whom to Ask and Where to Trade

Many people who handle their own investments also have a financial adviser—a security blanket of sorts, or a whipping post, depending on how the market is doing.

Decide how much hand holding you want and need, then start thinking about whether you want to work with someone on a fee or a commission basis. The fee basis gets a flat rate. With a commission agreement, your adviser makes money on everything he or she sells to you, or for you. There are also growing numbers of gurus and pundits, many of whom will sell you their picks and ideas if you subscribe to a newsletter or a Web site.

It's also handy to know the differences among stock exchanges. They're not all alike. Listing requirements are different, both qualitatively and quantitatively. There's a fundamental difference between the companies you'll find on the Nasdaq and on the New York Stock Exchange—never mind the electronic bulletin board.

Stock exchanges are sort of like private clubs. The stocks listed are "members" of these clubs and had to meet the requirements for joining as well as for continuing to remain members in good standing. But some clubs have stricter standards than others. A little exchange savvy can be helpful in deciding how much risk one stock may hold.

In the United States, there are three principal stock exchanges: (1) the New York Stock Exchange, (2) the Nasdaq Stock Market, and (3) the American Stock Exchange. In addition, many stocks trade or are quoted via the NASD Over-The-Counter Bulletin Board (OTCBB), the "pink sheets," and regional stock exchanges such as the Boston, Philadelphia, Pacific, and Midwest stock exchanges.

For decades, the New York Stock Exchange was the flagship trading platform for U.S. markets—and the exclusive home of the companies listed on the well-known Dow Jones Industrial Average. But the growing importance of technology in the world's economy has shifted much of the focus to the Nasdaq Stock Market, the wellspring of technologies issues. The Nasdaq actually is made up of two exchanges: the National Market and the Small Cap Market. The National Market is comprised of over 4,400 companies, including those well-known tech leaders we keep hearing about. The Small Cap includes about 1,800 mostly obscure companies. Each exchange has different entry and maintenance requirements for listed companies.

A Quote by Any Other Name

The Internet has done for stock quotes what Henry Ford did for automobiles: made them accessible to the masses. Every day, billions of shares—in more than 10,000 different stocks—trade in U.S. markets alone.

Pre-1996, most investors relied on the daily stock quote pages in their local newspapers. These day-old quotes provided a bare-bones snapshot of each company's trading history and current price-related information, but they were limited by the amount of paper and ink any reasonable publisher would commit. Therefore, thousands of mostly smaller company stocks were excluded.

The Internet knows no such barrier. Bytes are cheap and so are stock quotes. Even better, most quote engines provide a lot more data than just a current quote. Intraday highs and lows, volume, number of trades, charts, earnings, and much more data can often be found on most quote servers.

Because the stock quotes themselves are owned by the exchanges and then licensed to various sites or other media, the bulk of free quote servers provides quotes that are delayed by 15 to 20 minutes from the actual time of the last trade or the last quoted prices. These quotes are more than adequate for 90 percent of online quote queries.

Company News

Once upon a time—before the Internet—news stories about stocks and public companies were distributed principally through newspapers, magazines, television, and very expensive professional wire services. Additionally, any potential news story or company press release first met with the scrutiny of a trained financial editor. Most were simply ignored. Investors saw only the top stories.

The Internet has changed all that. With the Internet, everyone is his or her own gatekeeper and can let in whatever is of interest at the moment, with little regard for its origins.

Today, any company, individual, or organization—small, large, new, seasoned, inexperienced, or even fraudulent—can easily distribute instantly, to millions, its news, opinion, or information about any stock or public company. Message boards, chat rooms, Web sites, and e-mail are all vehicles to spread information that can affect markets, stocks, and the fortunes of individual investors.

Stockbrokers

In spite of the democratizing effects of modern online trading, stockbrokers remain a dominant force in the market. Over half of all trades are conducted by a full-service broker or a money manager.

Institutions and wealthy individuals don't always have the time or inclination to manage their own portfolios. And if you really aren't sure of what you're doing, then neither should you.

Brokers provide professional guidance and help select investments that are appropriate for each individual investor. They are bound to legal and ethical requirements of prudent advice and honest service. In return, the client pays a higher transaction fee or commission.

Most full-service stockbrokers earn a living by receiving a percentage of the trading and sales commissions their clients generate. This in turn fosters a natural conflict of interest between the broker, who is acting as an adviser, and his or her client. If the adviser has potential financial gain based on a recommendation to the client, that earnings potential may have affected his or her choice of investment.

Simply put, some brokers are better or more honest than others. All brokers are regulated, but some skirt ethical boundaries and are responsible for enormous fraud and investors' losses.

Never accept a recommendation from a cold-call stock-broker, especially on a stock that you've never heard of and haven't researched on your own. Boiler room brokers—those that prey on naïve investors and employ hard-sell or high-pressure sales tactics—are usually peddling the riskiest, if not the most fraudulent, stocks.

Stock Research

Every investor should do some research before buying shares in a company or mutual fund. The problems are (1) the enormous amount of research out there and (2) the high percentage of information that is flawed or even fraudulent. The trick is in knowing what you're using.

More and more investors are doing their own research via objective and not so objective sources of information. But brokerage research is still a powerhouse on The Street, even for those who don't have full-service accounts. Analysts' ratings can have a tremendous effect on a stock's fortunes.

Brokerage Research

There are dozens of full-service brokerage firms in the United States. All of the major nationwide firms and many of the larger regional and local ones offer their customers stock research. You can also find their research on the Internet or subscribe to services that aggregate or digest research from various firms.

Brokerages employ analysts who cover certain stocks or industries and periodically publish lengthy detailed reports about those companies or industries, along with the analysts' opinions about the prospects for investors. In connection with those reports, the firm will publish its recommendation to investors to buy, sell, or hold the company's shares, and will predict what the firm believes will be the future price of the stock.

Brokerage research can be quite useful; it often influences investors' perceptions. A favorable recommendation from a large and widely followed brokerage firm or analyst often results in an increase in the price of a stock.

Brokerage analysts are generally well trained and quite thorough in their analyses, but they cannot predict anything with certainty. They are often loath to make sell recommendations that may run contrary to the interests of the firm's clients, which may include the very companies that are the subjects of those reports.

Brokerage reports are not generally available to the public. Full-service brokerage firms spend a lot of money on this research and reserve the privilege for their own clients. However, you can get most of these reports for a fee (and some for free) from services that distribute brokerage research. Additionally, the highlights of a lot of this research, including the earnings estimates, price targets, and buy, sell, or hold recommendations, are available free or at fairly low cost on several popular Web sites.

Performance, Please

At the end of the day, investing is about how much money is made (or lost). Performance statistics jump at us from mutual funds, newsletter advertising, and even the pages of this book. And we're constantly being admonished (with good reason) that "Past performance is not a guarantee of future results."

Remember, performance stats, like any other statistics, can sometimes be misleading. For example, a mutual fund with high turnover could cause a greater taxable event to its shareholders than another fund with the same annual return but fewer turnovers. And inflation affects everyone by diminishing buying power.

Financial Statements: Everything You Wanted to Know but Were Afraid to Ask

At the heart of stock market research is the fundamental analysis of companies based on their financial condition and performance. Even in these times of confounding Internet and technology high-fliers, sales growth, earnings, profits, and losses remain relevant.

Brokerages and large investment institutions employ researchers and analysts who spend countless hours poring over details of companies' earnings reports, financial statements, and SEC filings. The massive flow of information on the Internet also makes much of this body of research and data available to investors. But a lot of it is full of technical and legal jargon, and most investors find it difficult to comprehend.

Common Sense

Never buy an unfamiliar stock because of unverified news or tips. This is akin to playing the lottery or gambling in Las Vegas. If the news is unverified, there's no way to know whether it's correct or even truthful.

Always regard greed and emotion as your enemies. Don't marry a stock. Emotion and ego are among the most expensive vices known. If you fell in love with a company, without knowing its vision, product, or management, get a mental divorce ASAP. This is about money. If you invest and then discover something about the company that might have prevented you from investing, then strongly consider getting out.

Dollar cost averaging doesn't always work. Dollar cost averaging is a simple strategy: You buy shares of stocks or mutual funds from time to time, regardless of price changes. As an example, suppose you purchase $1,000 of a stock at 10, then, subsequently, you buy more shares at 9, 11, 8, and 6. Your average share price is $8.42. Dollar cost averaging takes advantage of temporary downswings in the price of a stock or a fund in order to gain leverage and to make a larger profit by selling at a later date when the price is higher. This theory has one really fatal flaw. It assumes that the price of the subject stock or fund will increase again after having fallen below the initial purchase price. If you try dollar cost averaging on a stock that has begun to decline and does not recover, you'll only lose more money.

Nevertheless, dollar cost averaging is a generally sound theory. Historically, the markets, as measured by the S&P 500, have enjoyed a long-term pattern of price fluctuations with overall appreciation.

Reverse Mergers

If you are inclined to speculate in the realm of high-risk OTCBB and Nasdaq SmallCap stocks, you're likely to come across a company or two that became publicly traded not as a result of an initial public offering (IPO), but through what is commonly known as a reverse merger. These companies often present special risks to investors.

An IPO reveals a vast amount of financial disclosure and details in the circulated material (i.e., the prospectus). Other companies become public by simply merging with or acquiring the shell or remains of an idle or bankrupt, but publicly traded company. The add-ons, or merged companies, may be well-intended, cash-starved start-ups that are seeking a faster and lower-cost alternative to the IPO. Or they may be cleverly disguised scams targeted at investors.

A reverse merger typically occurs when a publicly traded company acquires a private company that is larger or more valuable than itself. The public company issues a majority or controlling number of shares to the company being acquired. Afterward, the acquired company becomes the controlling business; hence the term *reverse merger.*

Reverse mergers can offer private companies or start-ups an inexpensive way to become public and attract new investment capital. Unfortunately, because they are relatively inexpensive and skirt much regulatory scrutiny, scammers often use them to rip off investors.

Clues to those risks are buried in the fine details of the agreement that created the merger. Special research and a little common sense can help you wade through these stock scenarios and avoid companies that may present potential fraud.

The first detail you should pay attention to is whether a company did indeed go public via a merger rather than an IPO. To simplify things, make sure that the company you're investigating either had a true IPO or became public by some other means at least two years before. If that company is essentially the same operating business today that it was two years ago, there probably isn't much need for concern about whether it became public via a non-IPO method such as a reverse merger. Most reverse merger scams run their course within a year or two.

But if the company has had a substantial change in control, share capitalization, name, or core operating business within the past two years, it's time to do some careful research.

Most reverse mergers involve a "shell"—a publicly traded company that no longer has any significant operations or assets. Typically, such a company once had thriving business operations and is still publicly traded. It has a ticker symbol, one or more market makers, a name, and perhaps some trading activity from time to time. It may file an annual report of its financial condition with the SEC.

Legitimately, a start-up or a small operating business would value a publicly traded shell as an alternative to an expensive and uncertain IPO, and as a way to become a public company and raise investment capital. The shell could reasonably be worth $50,000 to $200,000, depending on its condition and the current demand for shells. Unfortunately, many reverse mergers are simply the foundation for micro-stock fraud. Unscrupulous conspirators use the shell as a vehicle for acquiring cheap and freely trading shares in anticipation of orchestrating a pump 'n' dump scheme.

What is the best way to know whether a reverse merger stock is a struggling but honest upstart or the next pull-the-wool-over-the public's-eyes pump 'n' dump? Dig into the company's financial statements and SEC filings. Look for any preexisting conditions or recent transactions that would add a significant number of freely trading shares to the company's float, at prices below the current share price.

Look for issuance of shares for consulting fees to persons or entities, or assets that may be of questionable value. If the shell paid 1 million shares, worth $5 each, for a technology patent of indeterminate value, you may want to consider whether that was a guise for issuing cheap stock to be sold to investors at a later date.

Most stock issued in a reverse merger is simply granted by the company and not subject to registration under an SEC or state securities filing. Such shares are restricted from public trading for at least one year. They are then exempt from registration, and, under SEC Rule 144, become free-trading shares that can be sold to the public. Watch out for companies that seem eager to promote themselves exactly one year after issuing a large amount of stock in exchange for little or no cash or tangible assets.

Beware of reverse mergers in which more than 5 percent of the surviving company's share capital remains in the hands of investors from the predecessor company or the shell. For example, suppose a shell consisting of 1 million free-trading shares issues an additional 9 million restricted shares to acquire an operating or start-up company that has "high hopes for the future." The new company begins life with 10 million shares outstanding. The successor company is 90 percent owned by the shareholders of the company that was acquired, and 10 percent by the shareholders of the shell. This leaves some questions to be answered.

1. Was the shell worth 10 percent of the successor company? If the successor company was a start-up with little or no operations or assets, then maybe it's a fair value for shareholders of the shell who sold their controlling interest to the acquired company. But if the acquired company is ten times more valuable than the shell, some people got a bum deal and maybe you shouldn't share in their poor judgment.

2. Who actually owns those shares from the shell and how may they benefit from their sale in the public market? In the reverse merger described above, chances are that the 9 million shares issued to the stockholders of the acquired company are not freely tradable; they are restricted from sale to the public for one to two years. Companies cannot just issue free-trading stock willy-nilly. Shares issued to insiders, affiliates, and investors who control 5 percent or more of the company's outstanding shares are subject to various disclosure and sale restrictions. They, along with other noninsider or noncontrolling shareholders, are further restricted from selling any shares not registered for public sale with the SEC. Most insiders are restricted for two years, and others are restricted for one year, under what is generally known as SEC Rule 144.

So that probably leaves most of the remaining 1 million shares owned by the shell shareholders in the public float and freely trading. But who are those shareholders? The typical method of the shell scammers is to acquire the freely trading shares of the shell very inexpensively, then merge with a company, promote its story and stock to the investing public, and sell those shares at greatly inflated prices before the restricted shareholders ever get a chance to sell.

The key to every successful stock scam is turning cheap or worthless paper into cash. Scammers view stock certificates as a kind of currency and the public company as the mint. The goal is to accumulate as much stock as possible, then exchange it for cash through sales to unsuspecting investors.

The many different ways for scammers to acquire shares include purchasing them in the open market. Securities regulations create certain obstacles, but there are enough ways for scammers to achieve their goals.

Acquiring cheap stock can be as simple as buying shares in low-priced stocks in the open market and then hyping those stocks. When other investors buy enough shares and drive prices high enough, the scammers can sell at a profit. This method is seldom employed by professional stock scammers but often is the approach used by amateurs. With the rise of Internet-based consumer-to-consumer communications, such as stock message boards, a lot more amateurs are out there.

Scams can be far more complicated, too. Scammers have found many creative means to acquire their shares. Sometimes they simply get favorable treatment under legitimate underwritings. At other times, they are paid in stock as consultants, or they gain control through corporate reorganizations or reverse mergers. The key to understanding the potential amount of stock controlled by scammers is to get as accurate an accounting as possible of all the company's share issuances.

Much of this information is disclosed in a company's initial and annual audited financial statements to the SEC (Form 10K or 10K-SB). More specifically, important information disclosing the dates, amounts, and other details of shares of stock issued by a company can be found in financial statements under the heading Shareholders' Equity and in the accompanying notes to the financial statements. Other financial statements or SEC filings, such as Forms S-8, S-1, SB-2, and so on, may disclose details of stock issuances.

504 Offerings

Reserved for small company offerings under $1 million per annum, shares issued under Section 504 are exempt from registration and can be freely traded in the open market very quickly. While Section 504 is often used legitimately by small companies to raise vital operating capital, it is also an easy tool for manipulators to use to obtain free trading shares dirt-cheap. Look for potentially unscrupulous 504 offerings when the price of the shares relative to the trading price of the stock is at a substantial discount compared to market price. There may be a manipulation planned.

For example, a public company, with 5 million shares outstanding, issues another 1 million shares in a 504 offering for about ten cents each, realizing $100,000 in capital raised. Subsequently, the company, or a third party on behalf of the company, initiates a promotional campaign which stimulates investor interest in its shares causing those shares to rise in price and volume. The resulting increase in price and volume provides the liquidity for the holders of the 1 million shares issued under the 504 to sell those shares often for much higher prices than they were recently purchased. After the promotional campaign ceases to cause investor demand for the company's shares, typically the price and volume wither away, leaving investors who purchased those shares in the open market with substantial losses.

Shares Issued for Acquisitions

Among scammers, a neat way to manufacture stock is to have a public company issue a whole lot of shares for some dubious assets. Such shares would generally not be registered immediately, but they are at least issued and could be sold privately to investors who are willing to wait a while before they can trade them. These shares would be registered at a later date by the company or become free trading after a holding period.

The Five Percent Solution

Here's one way that scammers often get around the reporting and trading restrictions reserved for insiders and large shareholders. The trick here is never to own more than 5 percent of a company's outstanding shares—at least not in one name. Most scammers, looking for big bucks, often acquire far more than 5 percent of a company's shares before hyping the stock and selling. However, when any investor—insider or otherwise—acquires more than 5 percent of a company's shares, he or she is subject to certain reporting requirements, or to restrictions on the number of shares that can be sold during a given time period. The scammers often solve this problem by simply spreading their holdings across numerous accounts under different individual and corporate names. Ultimately, these shill accounts are surreptitiously controlled by the beneficiary(ies) of the scam. Their control is often difficult to prove but easy to profile. Beware of large stock offerings for little cash, and of questionable services or acquisitions that appear to be spread too widely or to the point where there are few or no 5 percent (or larger) shareholders. Usually, in very young start-ups, the founders own much of the company's outstanding shares. When start-ups appear to have no founders owning a majority or a substantial stake in the enterprise, and the rest of the shares appear to have been issued for very little cash or valuable assets, be very cautious—if not outright skeptical—of the intentions.

The statement of cash flow is an exceptionally useful tool for investors who are inclined to dig a little deeper into a company's financial statements. All companies that report their financial condition to the SEC must adhere to standardized accounting methods. Income and loss statements are presented on an accrual basis and a company's reported earnings or losses can include large noncash items that may have a misleading appearance. The statement of cash flow is a reconciliation of noncash transactions with cash-based transactions. First and foremost, the statement tells how much money the company really earned or lost during the reporting period.

For example, if a company lands a large order, it may begin reporting that sale as income, even though it has not yet collected payment. On the statement of cash flow, accounts receivable are subtracted and accounts payable are added back in.

Among less scrupulous companies, accounts receivable are often the focus of inflated earnings statements. Pay special attention to them.

Chapter

3

THE SEC AND YOU

Spurred by the stock market crash of 1929 and the Great Depression that followed, Congress set up a system for regulating both the issuance and the trading of securities. The U.S. Securities and Exchange Commission (SEC) was established to enforce the rules laid out in the Securities Act of 1933 and the Securities and Exchange Act of 1934. The SEC was charged with an enormous task. Besides overseeing the new legislation, it would have to restore investors' confidence in a market that had rendered worthless half of the $50 billion in securities issued between the end of World War I and the 1929 crash.

More than 70 years later, personal memories of the Great Depression linger in the minds of our oldest citizens. Baby Boomers grew up hearing tales of that era and its hardships, but, for most people under 40, the Crash and its aftermath are nothing but folklore.

Too bad; they might have the most to lose.

On the up side, this segment of the population is the most computer savvy, and the SEC operates one of the most up-to-date online government sites. So, with just a little initiative, investors can look up most of the information needed to make sound investment decisions. The SEC's EDGAR (Electronic Data Gathering and Retrieval) database gives investors access to all company information filed electronically with the SEC since 1994. With a few keystrokes, investors can quickly find financial statements, notices of important events, and minutiae so arcane that one wonders why *anyone* would care. One missing item is Form 144 filings, which involve exemptions for unregistered securities. These are not filed electronically and cannot be found on the government site. But don't worry; there are other ways to find this information—some of it free but not timely, and some of it for a modest fee.

SEC filings are the definitive source of company information. If the information is not accurate, it had better not be in there.

Even if you plan to base all your investment decisions strictly on outside analyses—newsletters, brokers, hacks—a primer on EDGAR documents is essential for anyone in the market.

Leaving the heavy number crunching for someone else to sweat over is fine. But you should at least understand what your broker is telling you when he or she calls late in the trading day and is simply rabid about getting you 1,000 shares of so-and-so.

Learning even the basics about the treasure trove of SEC documents will not only make you a better investor, it will probably help you sleep at night. Delving into one of these lengthy, jargon-riddled filings is a match for the strongest double espresso.

But don't be put off. It's important stuff.

Where to Find It

The Securities and Exchange Commission requires all companies publicly traded in the United States to file certain information with it, electronically, on a regular basis. *Electronically* is the key word here. Until about five years ago, the only way to get your hands on these documents was through a company itself, or by snail mail from the SEC.

Since the Internet took over as the cheapest and fastest means of communication and transmission of this much data anyone with online access can dig up even obscure information about any publicly traded firms. And if you're really good, you can do it in less time than a typical metropolitan commute.

The SEC maintains these documents on its site, which is free: http://www.sec.gov/cgi-bin/srch-edgar. The revamped version of the government site is a vast improvement, both in load time and navigation, over the site that was originally launched.

But it's still pretty bare bones. Plug in a company's name (not the ticker symbol; for some reason, that won't work) and you'll get a menu of filings, along with the data and the size of the file (bytes, kilobytes).

Many finance-oriented sites will give you access to EDGAR documents through one interface or another. Your broker's Web site is usually a good place to look for a link. But there are several sites at which the sole focus is EDGAR, as their names reflect:

- EDGAR Online http://www.edgar-online.com and Free EDGAR http://www.freeedgar.com.
- EDGAR Online, is a subscription service. Fees range from about $15 per quarter to $100 per month. One of the big differences here is that EDGAR Online offers access to real-time filings, including Form 144 filings, which track insider trading and the sale of other unregistered securities. Other sites make Form 144 filings available free, but they can be anywhere from a few days to a few weeks old before getting posted.

- Free EDGAR, like the SEC, is a nonsubscription site that's pretty easy to navigate. It offers users a watch list where they can enter the symbols of their favorite stocks and receive a notification, via e-mail, whenever any of those companies files a document with the SEC.

Learning how to decipher EDGAR filings is one of the most important elements of the Stock Detective's method of determining whether an investment is a good risk.

A glossary of all of the SEC's forms is in Appendix B. The forms can be accessed through the SEC's site or one of the other EDGAR portals.

The SEC has a form for just about anything, from changing accountants (Form 8-K) to whether a CEO is doing business with his mother (Proxy, DEF 14A). Of the approximately 300 forms, here are the ones you'll want to pay attention to on a regular basis.

Forms 10 and 10-SB. This is an initial registration statement. Companies file it when they are reporting to the SEC for the first time. A mudslide of these documents was filed after regulators started requiring bulletin board companies to file full reports in 1999. These filings are essentially the same as a company's annual financial statements on Form 10K, but they are the *initial* audited financial statements of the subject company, and they include interim as well as annual financial statements depending on the date filed.

SB denotes a "small business filing." The necessary information is essentially the same as for larger businesses, but fewer details are required.

Forms 10-K and 10-KSB (Annual Report). These are among the most in-depth documents on the face of the earth. Companies must detail their business: how they stack up against the competition; finances; who and what all of its subsidiaries are; and an honest guess at how any ongoing litigation they are involved in might turn out. A firm's organizational structure is outlined, and its officers and directors are briefly profiled. Financial information includes two years of audited balance sheets, and audited income statements for the most recent fiscal year.

Forms 10-Q and 10-QSB (Quarterly Report). This is a much shorter version of the company's annual report. One of the big differences is that the financial information in a Form 10-Q does not have to be audited. This form must be filed within 45 days of the quarter's close. In addition to the unaudited financials, Form 10-Q must report any legal proceedings and material changes in the company's operations. These could include changes among subsidiaries, long-term contracts, or other events that could have a long-term effect on the company's well-being.

Form 8-K. One of the Stock Detective's favorite red flags is a change in auditors. Here's where you'll find that kind of event—quickly. Companies must report any significant change in its ownership or financial situation within 15 days on a Form 8-K. That includes not only changing auditors (Did the earlier ones quit because they wouldn't agree to certain accounting procedures?), but changes in ownership, sales, or acquisitions involving other companies (including their financial statements), and bankruptcy proceedings.

Proxy, DEF 14A. The main purpose of a proxy statement is to tell shareholders what issues they'll be voting on at an upcoming shareholders' meeting. It also lists salaries of certain corporate officers and details any family ties that affect business transactions.

Prospectus. Investors who are considering investing in a new company should always request a prospectus, even if the company is new only to them. A prospectus, in many ways, is a wish list with certain legal restrictions attached. Companies must issue a prospectus whenever they plan to put new shares up for public sale. Through the prospectus, the company lays out its long-term goals, tells how it plans to achieve them, and points to what it has done in the past that should inspire investors' confidence that it can, in fact, perform. It must also explain how it will use the money raised through the stock sale. If you latch onto a prospectus that's a year old, study it to gauge how well the company is meeting the goals that were stated at the time of the offering.

Form 144. Anyone who is holding unregistered, or restricted, shares in a company and wishes to sell them under the exemption provided by Rule 144 must file Form 144 with the SEC. The form signals an insider's *intention* to sell, not the actual sale. It also serves as a onetime exemption from registration for the number of shares identified in the filing. Form 144 must be filed if more than 500 shares are sold within a three-month period, or if the aggregate sale price of the shares sold during that time is more than $10,000.

If you're trying to figure out how a number of people are involved across multiple companies, try the 10K Wizard, http://10kwizard.com. Plug in a name, and the site will pull up all of the SEC filings in which that name appears. And if you're confused and frustrated when you see the amended filing to a 600-page Form 10K, don't despair. Instead, check out The Herring Inspector at http://www.herringinspector .com, which allows you to compare two documents with just a couple of keystrokes. The free version will compare the first 500 lines of two documents. If you want more details, or a lengthy comparison, you will have to subscribe. But the fee is only $12 a year.

Other Information on the SEC Site

If you're tired of plodding through EDGAR filings, there's plenty of other information on its Web site that the SEC would just love to have every investor ponder.

Litigation releases (http://www.sec.gov/enforce/litig.htm). Although stretched thin, the SEC's legal staff maintains a pretty steady stream of litigation. Investors can keep track of the legal comings and goings among the agency's enforcement division through the Litigation Releases section of the site. The area is updated roughly on a weekly basis, and provides a summary of all legal action that the SEC has initiated, settled, or participated in. A section of the site culls out the Internet-related actions and lists them separately.

Daily summaries (http://www.sec.gov/ndighome.htm). If you're eager to find the disposition of a particular case the SEC has pending, check the daily summaries. This area contains new information on a variety of housekeeping items (Investment Company Act releases, Securities Act registrations, and proposed rules that self-regulatory organizations are submitting to the SEC). It is also the first place enforcement proceedings are posted.

Investor education (http://www.sec.gov/oiea1.htm). The SEC's investor education site is generic but comprehensive. It covers the basics on how to invest, gives tips for trading online, and devotes a section to cyber fraud alerts, allowing investors to keep tabs on the latest scams. A mutual fund calculator and a retirement estimator are among the interactive tools that are offered.

Brokerage firms' Web sites offer investor education information and tools similar to the SEC's offerings. But there is a growing debate over whether brokers—both full-service and discount—should be required to provide investor education— and if so, how much.

There's no disagreement on whether investors should be educated. The question is: How? Brokers are leery of being too intrusive—having windows pop up at certain steps in the research or trading process, for example. That would undermine the present attraction of online trading—it's self-directed and fast. Brokers also want to keep investors visiting their site; they are resistant to hyperlinking them to a neutral third party such as the SEC.

In true bureaucratic fashion, the SEC and participants in its 1999 roundtable discussion on what trading will look like in the future, agreed to study how investors use educational material provided through online brokerage firms. Stay tuned.

Even a little education can go a long way, because investors are their own best defense against fraud.

Companies try all kinds of schemes and ruses to get away with an amazing variety of tricks. Some are bold, some are simply stupid, but most are detectable if you play by the Stock Detective's rules.

False Statements, Imaginary Revenue, and Other Loose Interpretations of GAAP

Believe it or not, people actually make stuff up and file it with the SEC. It's almost impossible to tell, simply by looking, whether an entry on a financial statement or in an annual report is fictitious. If you're really serious about investing in a company that's had little verifiable independent research done by analysts, pick up the phone. If the company claims to have a contract with so-and-so, call so-and-so and find out whether it's true.

You might be surprised by what you find out.

Take, for example, Peritus Software Services, Inc. During the second quarter of 1998, the Massachusetts firm reported revenue of more than $1 million attributed to a software license it had sold to AT&T. This report boosted the company's revenue at least 10 percent for that quarter. However, there was no license, and therefore no revenue, according to the SEC, which charged Peritus's CFO and an account manager with fraud.

According to the SEC, the men charged in the case, "In order to substantiate Peritus' claim to the revenue, . . . falsely told Peritus' director of finance and its controller, as well as its outside auditors, that AT&T Corp. had purchased the license pursuant to a $1.9 million purchase order, and that Peritus had delivered the software to AT&T." Without admitting or denying the allegations, Peritus agreed to an order entered by the SEC. The CFO and account manager were sanctioned and fined.

Fabricating a contract with a blue-chip company like AT&T might seem, at first, like a bad choice. But, considering the psychological and logistical factors involved, it's actually quite clever. Simply using a big name gives a scam artist a certain credibility. Seeing Peritus and AT&T mentioned together, in an SEC document, would send many investors straight to their E*Trade account. Even skeptics would have a hard time debunking this contract. How easy would it be to track down the one or two people out of AT&T's 147,000 employees who actually can confirm or deny its existence? A lot harder than if you were calling a much smaller establishment, where one or two people know ALL of the company's contracts.

And in an auditing and enforcement proceeding against Peritus, the "Commission found that Peritus' internal controls did not ensure that software had been delivered before recognizing revenue on the sale of a software license." This is another item that should be on the investigative investor's checklist. A company that doesn't have a solid internal control system presents unscrupulous insiders with all kinds of opportunities.

Gene Didonato, Peritus's general counsel, said the company's settlement with the SEC prevented him from commenting directly on the case. But he pointed to the company's most recently filed 10-K and 10-Q for examples of how Peritus addressed the internal controls issue.

"A control has been added to the revenue recording process to confirm software delivery prior to revenue. In addition, a software receipt acknowledgement signed by the customer is generally obtained to confirm software delivery. The Company's legal staff is now responsible for informing the finance staff of any acceptance conditions contained within any contract. The finance staff is now responsible for ensuring any acceptance conditions are met prior to revenue recording. Finally, the Company's Chief Financial Officer reviews all significant revenue transactions for proper recording," Peritus's March 30, 2000, 10-K says.

This illustrates one of the big "qualitative" differences between OTCBB and Nasdaq listed companies. Even though both are presently subject to the same financial reporting standards of the SEC, the NASD goes a step further and requires its members to meet certain standards, including internal record-keeping controls and corporate governance rules. For example, the NASD requires member companies to have an independent "audit committee" that includes outside directors. Another factor is the selection of the auditor. There's no rule that says a company has to have a "Big Five"-quality auditor, but some companies have unqualified or fraudulent auditors who either "look the other way" or actually conspire to misstate these companies' finances.

Inventory and Cash Flow Problems

A company's inventory represents several things, including potential future revenue and any current liability. And there are different types of inventory. First determine whether the company is a manufacturer, supplier, or retailer. Each will have different supply needs.

For example, a manufacturing firm will have inventories of raw materials, supplies, goods in production, and finished products ready for sale. Suppliers will deal almost exclusively in raw materials. Retailers' stockpiles will consist entirely of finished goods.

In any of these instances, tracking a company's inventory over several quarters can help identify future problems.

Inventories should remain fairly steady, unless a product is seasonal or large contracts are due to be fulfilled in the next quarter or two. When inventories inexplicably spike up, it could indicate either that sales have slowed considerably, or other problems on the distribution end.

Two other entries on the balance sheet should also be reviewed: line of credit and accounts payable. A significant increase in either could spell cash flow problems. An increase in both during roughly the same time period is a warning sign.

A tough quarter for accounts payable shouldn't shake an investor. But a pattern of excessive unpaid bills could indicate a problem. Why haven't the bills been paid? There are legitimate reasons—a disputed or unfinished contract might cause a company to withhold payment. Or perhaps the supplier simply doesn't want to be paid until a later time (in which case, investors might want to scrutinize that company's books to see whether it's scooting revenue around).

More than likely, however, an escalating accounts payable entry indicates cash flow problems. And where there's a lack of cash, there's usually trouble. It can come in several forms: increased debt, or line of credit, simply to fund operations; issuing more shares to raise operating capital, thus diluting current shareholders' value; or creative accounting measures that may mask a problem until it's too late for most investors to bail out.

An increasing line of credit is not necessarily a bad thing. It could mean a company's finances are so strong that it can now borrow from reputable creditors at attractive rates. But it can also mean that it's strapped for cash and has been forced to go into a usurious market simply to continue operating. If you can't be sure which situation applies, read the SEC filing carefully. Make sure you can determine who the creditor is and what the terms of the loan are. These facts may not always be spelled out in the document's narrative. Instead, you may have to turn to what is often an EDGAR filing's gold mine—the footnotes.

Investors need to pay attention to another issue when credit, or debt, is involved. Look more closely if a company starts retiring debt early, especially if it's cheap debt. Why would a firm pay off a loan that burns a mere 6 percent interest, when it could instead use those funds for research, capital expenditures like equipment, or marketing—any of which could yield a higher return than the interest cost.

Paying off debt is not always a warning sign. A company may want to "strengthen its balance sheet" and replace the debt capital with an equity offering—on which it does not pay any interest. That could potentially improve the company's cash flow by eliminating its debt service, and increase shareholder value by increasing its book value.

Issuing more shares to raise capital is not unusual; more often than not, it's a perfectly legitimate way to fund a growing company. But what does it mean for current investors? At least in the short term, it dilutes the value of their shares. If a company has 10 million shares outstanding, and you own 1 million, you've got a 10 percent stake. If the company issues another 10 million, your holdings dwindle to 5 percent. A more likely situation is that lower earnings per share will simply hurt individual investors. A $1 million profit spread across 10 million shares yields earnings per share (EPS) of 10 cents. Spread that across 20 million shares and the earnings go down to 5 cents.

Again, an equity offering is not always a bad thing. The reality is that growing companies need cash to continue to grow. And the new cash does a couple of things to offset dilution of earnings. For example, it may be invested (1) in expanding plant capacity to meet growing orders, thus increasing earnings, or (2) for an acquisition that increases assets and/or earnings. The cash received from the sale of stock is an asset on the balance sheet and contributes to the book value per share. Most companies' book value per share is far less than the market value of its stock. If the offering is made at the market price (as most secondary public offerings are), then in all likelihood it will improve book value per share after the dilution of new shares issued.

The most dangerous form of new stock issuances is a sale at a discount to the market price of the company's shares. Some sales are also done through convertible securities (they can convert into stock below the market price with or without limitation). Small companies often have to resort to selling shares below market because their stock prices are not characterized by any substantial liquidity and represent an unusual risk for those purchasing large amounts. In these companies, it is important to carefully examine the terms of such stock sales. If the shares are generally restricted from trading for a reasonable period of time, then it can be assumed that the company is protecting public shareholders' interests by making the private purchasers wait a while before they can sell. The biggest abuses are from discounted and convertible discounted offerings under Rule 504 (no waiting period) or

Regulation S, before the waiting period was extended to one year. Form S-8 can also foster abuse, when consultants are compensated as if they are employees and get fully registered shares in the filing.

The basic rule here is: Whenever a company creates a situation in which a large shareholder or a group of shareholders holds a large position at a discount to the market price and has the ability to sell those shares in the market, then there is a likelihood that those shares will be sold. And, given their lower cost basis, they are likely to sell at lower prices and depress the stock price. In another tricky scenario, companies may issue shares without registration but at very low prices or in exchange for questionable assets. Then they simply wait one year before promoting their stock so that the holders of the cheap stock can sell into the market.

Don't confuse this sequence with a stock split. Remember, with a forward split, investors maintain their relative position in the shareholder pecking order. Ten shares previously worth $2 apiece, for a total of $20, are now 20 shares at $1 apiece. The total value is still $20.

An excellent resource for those who want to learn more is *Financial Shenanigans: How to Detect Accounting Gimmicks & Fraud in Financial Reports,* by Howard M. Schilit.

Chapter

4

WHO ARE YOU UP AGAINST?

The bull market has spawned a new generation of stock hucksters. Who are they, where do they come from, and where are they likely to end up?

People behind shady stock deals come from all walks of life, but a heavy concentration has backgrounds in the securities industry—either as brokers or promoters.

But hucksters are by no means limited to these professions. As we'll soon see, even a tree trimmer can make a bundle if he or she has superior communications skills and a good Internet connection.

Paid Promoters

Stock promoters were once subject to the constraints of snail mail and an occasional radio spot. The Internet has practically given them a license to print stock certificates—cheap.

There is no official tally of the number of promoters out there, but a conservative estimate would put them at several hundred. Unlike financial advisers, they don't have to register with the SEC—or anyone else, for that matter—so long as they comply with whatever state and local rules govern their incorporation. Financial advisers, on the other hand, must file with state and federal agencies and are closely regulated.

Paid promoters, who don't always make it clear that they're paid to promote, make it abundantly clear that they are not doling out financial or investment advice.

The SEC requires anyone who is paid to promote a stock to fully disclose the terms, including the amount they are paid and in what form—usually, cash or stock. The SEC is very clear about this in Rule 17b.

Nonetheless, the rule is flouted daily by many promoters. Several SEC sweeps in recent years brought some promoters in line, but many still skirt the spirit of the law.

Rule 17b of the Securities Act of 1933 deals with fraudulent interstate transactions:

http://www.law.uc.edu/CCL/33Act/sec17.html

Use of interstate commerce for purpose of offering for sale. It shall be unlawful for any person, by the use of any means or instruments of transportation or communication in interstate commerce or by the use of the mails, to publish, give publicity to, or circulate any notice, circular, advertisement, newspaper article, letter, investment service, or communication which, though not purporting to offer a security for sale, describes such security for a consideration received or to be received, directly or indirectly, from an issuer, underwriter, or dealer, without fully disclosing the receipt, whether past or prospective, of such consideration and the amount thereof.

The examples below are fairly typical of disclaimers an investor might find on a tout site, if he or she bothers to look. Only a small fraction of the paid promoters operating on the Internet put their disclaimer information front and center. In most cases, visitors to the site have to actually seek out the disclaimer link and then read the super-tiny fine print.

Notice in Example 1 that the company says that just about anyone associated with it—employees, clients, officers, directors, and their families—"may from time to time purchase, be compensated by, or otherwise hold positions in securities of the companies featured [on the company's site]." But there are no specifics regarding compensation. Either this tout is really bad and can't get anyone to pay for hyping the stock, or the SEC's dictum on disclosing how much they were paid is being ignored.

But it gets worse. The second half of that sentence—"any such positions may be increased or decreased in the future"— pretty much tells investors that this crew is ready to dump their cheaply acquired shares just as soon as they've pumped the market high enough.

Example 1

Disclaimer:

The comments, financial profiles, corporate and product profiles and opinions expressed on this web site are those of our featured companies and although deemed reliable, the accuracy and reliability of those sources are not guaranteed.

The opinions and comments on this web site are not to be construed as an offer to sell or a solicitation to buy any securities or investments mentioned herein. Affiliates, employees, clients, officers, directors and their families may from time to time purchase, be compensated by, or otherwise hold positions in securities of the companies featured on "this site" as agents or principals, and any such positions may be increased or decreased in the future. If there are any questions regarding this disclaimer please use our convenient e-mail to contact us at . . .

Example 2 comes at the end of a 3,000-words-plus e-mail. How many people actually get to the end of the text—which is more than twice as long as the average newspaper article, and an absolute epic compared to items in *USA Today*—is not clear. Our guess is: Not many.

But surfers who do stumble across this wordy bit of compliance might still have some trouble sorting out who's paying whom for what.

The first paragraph states that the promoter was paid thousands of shares of free-trading stock for its promotional efforts, and that it owns an additional several thousand shares, which it purchased on the open market. But scroll down a little farther and there's a disclaimer from another company, which says, way down at the very, very bottom, that if the promoter is ever compensated, the payment will be clearly identified. There's no explanation about what, if any, relationship promoter B has to promoter A, and this raises an abundance of questions: Are they affiliated? Is one a subsidiary of the other? Was promoter B paid through promoter A for the tout? If so, how many of the shares went to each promoter?

Example 2

Disclaimer:

Legal Disclosure

This publication is an advertisement for the Company whose articles and/or information appears herein and may not be construed as investment advice. All articles, notices, and other information contained herein concerning any featured Company are an advertisement for such Company. No analysis has been made by the Publisher of the financial position, condition, business, and other factors about the Company, which may appear in the advertisements contained herein. All information about the Company contained herein has been furnished by the respective Company, or by affiliates or consultants of the Company, and the Publisher has not made any independent verification of any such information. The information contained herein is based upon sources that we consider reliable but is not guaranteed by "the publisher" or its officers, directors, employees or any affiliated parties. Any sales and/or earnings forecasts included herein were obtained by and/or from financial statements and/or news releases and unless otherwise stated are not endorsed by the management of the company which is the subject matter of this advertisement. The Publisher, therefore, makes no guarantee as to the reliability of such information. The advertisements are not a solicitation to purchase or hold, or dispose of stock securities of an advertising Company. Readers should consult with their own independent tax, business and financial advisors with respect to any investment opportunity, including any contemplated investment in the advertised Company. All information concerning a Company advertising herein and contained in this publication should be verified independently with such company and an independent securities analyst. The Publisher, its affiliates, officers, directors, subsidiaries and agents (collectively, "the Publisher") of this advertisement has been compensated by the "Company X" for distributing this advertisement. Compensation includes free trading shares of "XYZZZ." The Publisher also holds shares of stock in the Company, purchased in the open market. The Publisher will therefore benefit from an increase in share price of "the Company." The Publisher may sell these shares or purchase more shares in the Company at any time before, during or after the distribution of this advertisement. Facsimile reproduction of this advertisement is permitted provided that proper credit is given to the publisher, including the URL. "The publisher" distributes to countries around the world. If this publication contravenes any securities laws and/or regulations, the securities regulations of the country will prevail. In which case that this issue does offend such regulation this issue must be discarded.

Forward-Looking Statements

Safe Harbor for Forward-Looking Statements: Except for historical information contained herein, the statements on this website and newsletter are forward-looking statements that are made pursuant to the safe harbor provisions of the Private Securities Reform Act of 1995. Forward-looking statements involve known and unknown risks and uncertainties, which may cause a company's actual results in the future periods to differ materially from forecasted results. These risks and uncertainties include, among other things, product price volatility, product demand, market competition and risk inherent in the companies' operations. Included in this release are forward-looking statements within the meaning of Section 27A of the Securities Act of 1933, as amended, and Section 21E of the Securities Exchange Act of 1934, as amended. Although the Company believes that the expectations reflected in such forward-looking statements are reasonable, it can give no assurance that such expectations reflected in such forward-looking statements will prove to have been correct. The companies' actual results could differ materially from those anticipated in the forward-looking statements as a result of certain factors including sales levels, distributions and competition trends and other market factors.

DISCLAIMER

"Promoter B" is an electronic advertisement providing information on selected companies. All statements and expressions are the opinion of "promoter B" and are not meant to be either investment advice or a solicitation or recommendation to buy, sell, or hold securities. Readers are cautioned that small and micro-cap stocks are high-risk investments and that some or all investment dollars can be lost. We suggest you consult a professional investment advisor before purchasing any stock. All opinions expressed by "promoter B" are the opinions of "the promoter." All information is received directly from the companies profiled and/or outside interviews conducted by "the promoter." While "the promoter" believes its sources to be reliable, "the promoter," its officers, directors, employees or any affiliated parties make no representation or warranty as to the accuracy of the information provided. Readers should not rely solely on the information contained in this publication, but should consult with their own independent tax, business and financial advisors with respect to any investment opportunity, including any contemplated investment in the advertised Company(s).

We recommend you use the information found here or in our e-mail alerts as an initial starting point for conducting your own research and conduct your own due diligence (DD) on the featured companies in order to determine your own personal opinion of the company before investing in these or any other companies.

"The promoter" assumes all information to be truthful and reliable; however, we cannot warrant or guarantee the accuracy of this information. All statements contained herein or in our e-mail alerts are deemed to be factual as of the date of the report and as such are subject to change without notice. "The promoter" is not an Investment Advisor, Financial Planning Service or a Stock Brokerage Firm and in accordance with such "The promoter" is not offering investment advice or promoting any investment strategies. "The promoter" is not offering securities for sale or solicitation of any offer to buy or sell securities. An offer to buy or sell can be made only with accompanying disclosure documents and only in the states and provinces for which they are approved. Oftentimes "The promoter" receives cash or stock from a third party for the dissemination of its e-mail alerts. In the event "The promoter" receives compensation of any kind, that precise and exact form of compensation shall be clearly displayed in the disclaimer portion of the specific e-mail alert sent to all subscribers. When compensated, there is an inherent conflict of interest in "The promoter" statements and opinions and such statements and opinions cannot be considered independent. "The promoter" will benefit from any increase in the share price of said profiled stocks. "The promoter" may liquidate its position in the aforementioned profiled Companies at ANY time, before, during or immediately after the release of this stock profile.

Safe Harbor Disclosure:

Any and all "The promoter" stock profiles contain or incorporate by reference "forward-looking statements," including certain information with respect to plans and strategies of the featured company. As such, any statements contained therein or incorporated therein by reference that are not statements of historical fact may be deemed to be forward-looking statements. Without limiting the foregoing, the words "believe(s)," "anticipate(s)," "plan(s)," "expect(s)," "project(s)" "anticipate(s)" and similar expressions are intended to identify forward-looking statements. There are a number of important factors that could cause actual events or actual results of the Companies profiled herein to differ materially from these indicated by such forward-looking statements.

This particular e-mail newsletter uses another common tout tactic: a slightly twisted form of bait and switch.

Before delving into its current profile, Promoter B takes a moment to update readers on the performance of four other companies it has recently profiled.

Within two weeks of being spewed across the Internet in the promoters' e-mail hype, shares in each of these companies shot up dramatically on the OTC bulletin board. And that's what the promoter wants to tell investors. One company climbed 300 percent, a second bounced up 62 percent, another jumped 147 percent, and the last company leapt more than 100 percent.

Now, if you feel foolish for not buying each and every one of these companies when the promoter brought them to your attention, imagine how people who actually did buy them felt when the stocks started tanking.

The promoter forgot to mention that, despite the stupendous performance of each one of these darlings, there's a downside. By the time the e-mail heralding the stocks' grand performance was released, each one had lost a significant amount of its gains. And two were actually trading below pre-hype prices, even after adjusting for some pretty hefty splits.

At the end of both companies' disclaimers, note the arrogant phrase telling investors that they can and will sell their shares at any time, and, furthermore, that they stand to benefit from a rise in price, such as one that might be the result of the e-mail they are reading. In other words, the promoters are gonna scalp those shares, and they've given you fair warning.

Scalping

Nothing seems to quite raise the SEC's ire like scalping—selling stock on a price bounce that is at least partially due to the seller's own promotion of said shares. Even promoters who offer full disclosure of their compensation aren't immune to prosecution for scalping. And it happens a lot more often than most people might think.

Take the case of eConnect. According to the SEC, "a treetrimmer masquerading as a financial analyst" twice publicly issued recommendations to buy shares in this publicly traded company. The "analyst" touted eConnect as an undervalued company and projected a short-term "target" price of $12 to $25 a share and a one-year "target" price of $100 to $135 a share. The complaint further alleges that prior to issuing the recommendation, the "analyst" bought several thousand shares of eConnect stock. After his reports circulated, the "analyst" took advantage of the market interest he had created by selling his eConnect stock into the inflated market. The "analyst" failed to disclose that he owned large amounts of eConnect stock and that he intended to sell the stock in contravention of his buy recommendation—a fraudulent practice known as "scalping." According to the complaint, the "analyst realized profits of over $1.4 million from sales of eConnect stock." The "analyst" denied the allegation but his attorney declined to comment further.

The company and its president also faced civil charges from the SEC that accused them of "issuing false and misleading press releases (1) eConnect and its joint venture partner had a unique licensing arrangement with Palm, Inc., a manufacturer of hand-held personal computer products; and (2) a subsidiary of eConnect had a strategic alliance with a brokerage firm concerning a system that would permit cash transactions over the Internet. The Commission further alleged that eConnect had no licensing arrangement whatsoever with Palm, Inc., and the "strategic alliance" is no more than a letter of intent between a brokerage and a joint venture partner of eConnect. The complaint further alleged that the fraudulent press releases, which were disseminated through a wire service as well as by postings on Internet bulletin boards, caused a dramatic rise in the price of eConnect stock from $1.39 on February 28, 2000, to a high of $21.88 on March 9, 2000, on heavy trading volume."

Without admitting or denying the allegations, eConnect and its president accepted an order from the SEC which forbids them "from taking any action or making any statement, or failing to make any statement that would violate" certain securities laws. The attorney representing them on the SEC charges, said he's not sure the government's complaints about the press releases would have impressed a judge. But his clients settled the charges because it "was more important not to let this bring the company down. It was more important to move on with company business." "My clients never made a nickel. No one sold a single share of stock," the attorney said. "With the press releases in question, maybe they didn't describe the relationship perfectly. But I don't know that the judge would find that openly misleading."

The combination of the three contacts—e-mail, Web sites, and chat rooms/message boards—has been fertile ground for the SEC, which has filed charges against dozens of promoters since late 1998. And although many are shut down as a result of their tangle with the SEC, there's little or no gap while new ones sprout in their place.

One of the first to fall was a pioneer in the industry—a company (which shall remain nameless due to pending litigation) that opened up both the medium and the message.

The company set up shop in 1996 and recommended at least 25 microcap stocks to investors before it was caught up in an SEC sweep in October 1998. The company was estimated to have reached at least 100,000 people, including subscribers to its newsletter and visitors to its Web site. In its complaint against the company and its owner, the SEC said that every one of the 25 stocks recommended had a substantial price rise after being featured by the company, but then quickly sank, leaving many new investors with a substantial loss. If true, it was a classic pump 'n' dump maneuver. According to the SEC, not only did the company skip the SEC's disclosure requirement, it also failed to tell investors that although it was urging them to buy into these various microcap shares, the company-was dumping most of its holdings as quickly as possible, once the price started to climb.

Perhaps even more interesting, a former associate of the company made major headlines. In October 1999, one of the highest profile crimes in the penny stock industry rattled a tiny New Jersey community when Maier S. Lehmann and Alain Chalem were found slain, gangland style, in the dining room of Chalem's Colts Neck mansion.

The two men promoted stocks online via their site, stock-investor.com. This now-defunct site suspended operations shortly after their deaths, which many speculate were related to their involvement in the world of penny stocks. Lehmann had had several scrapes with the SEC, including the Commission's investigation of Electro-Optical, Inc., a client of the company discussed previously. The Massachusetts-based firm is no longer around, but its "assets" and some people who were involved with Electro-Optical, are now at the center of a $16 million, international fraud recovery effort by the SEC. Lehmann had agreed to pay $630,000 to settle charges that he had fraudulently promoted shares of Electro-Optical, Inc., which was hawking a fingerprint identification system. Throughout the months-long manipulation of Electro-Optical stock, a price spike was engineered that at one point equaled a 1,000 percent increase in a single day—from $0.25 per share to more than $5. The SEC suspended trading in Electro-Optical shares in March 1998, and it has since withered away to . . . that's right, an empty shell.

Investors who didn't live in the circulation area of the New Jersey newspapers covering the crime, needed to look no further than Silicon Investor's message boards, where more than 1,000 messages plotted out the murders, speculated on the motive, and even dabbled in suggesting suspects.

While technology is helping the SEC operate a little closer to Internet time, a lot of damage can still be done while regulators build a case sturdy enough to either halt trading or file a complaint.

By the time the NASD Regulation shut down Stratton Oakmont Securities Inc. in 1996, hundreds of investors had lost at least $7 million, according to court documents. Regulators breathed a sigh of relief when Stratton Oakmont's expulsion was announced:

> With this expulsion, NASD Regulation has rid the securities industry of one of its worst actors," said NASDR President Mary L. Schapiro. "With Stratton Oakmont's extensive and serious regulatory history, and an obvious disregard for all rules of fair

practice, today's actions make the securities industry a better place for investors.

In one of Stratton Oakmont's most egregrious acts, it underwrote an IPO for a company that raised almost $7 million. Of that amount, only $163,000 went to the company. Insiders pocketed the rest, according to a report by the New York State Attorney General.

But even though Stratton Oakmont and several of its principals were expelled and barred from the securities industry, the case had spawned hundreds of "brokers" who could take this poisonous game to new chop shops and boiler rooms. To help instill loyalty in its recruits, Stratton Oakmont used the firm to shield brokers from prosecution. With its "extensive and serious regulatory history," Stratton Oakmont had been defending itself against complaints and investigations for years. The firm usually settled arbitrations with a provision that complaints and charges against individual brokers were dismissed. This not only promoted loyalty, it gave brokers no reason to point fingers. So, when Stratton Oakmont went under, this well-trained army simply set out in search of new territories and recruits.

After the Fall

Trading suspensions are not very common. But they are often the death knell for companies that are booted off the bulletin board. Trading suspensions are almost exclusively enforced against thinly traded penny stocks.

According to the SEC, penny stock "generally refers to low-priced (below $5), speculative securities of very small companies." All penny stocks trade in the OTC Bulletin Board or the pink sheets, but not on national exchanges such as the New York Stock Exchange or the Nasdaq Stock Market. Penny stocks can't be sold to just anyone. A broker must determine that the client is suitable for such a risky investment (read: no nest-egg-only widows, please). The customer must agree to the transaction, in writing, after being told of the specific risks involved—again, in writing. Finally, the broker must tell the client how much he or she (or the firm) will be making on the penny stock sale. When the transaction is completed, the brokerage firm must send a monthly statement detailing the market value of every penny stock the client holds.

A number of criteria may get a stock halted. The most common holdup comes when false, misleading, or even questionable statements are made about projected earnings or potential sales. Another measure the SEC watches closely is trading *volume*, not just trading price. When a company that has barely been trading a couple thousand shares in a week suddenly churns out millions of shares in a day, the SEC tends to get curious.

In 1999, the SEC suspended trading in 21 stocks—double the average number of suspensions (11) for the previous three years. Of the 21 companies that had trading halted, only one later qualified to return to trading on the OTC Bulletin Board. A handful bounced around in the pink sheets, but most simply disappeared.

Pink Sheets

Suppose you are a true believer, and you are determined to invest in a company that has just come off a suspension. You are convinced that it has hit bottom and is on its way up. Trading in this company's shares will be difficult because brokers (those who are playing by the rules) can't quote a share price until they have in their possession a complete financial report from the company. They are complying with Rule 15c-211, the "blue sky" rule.

For most companies, a listing in Standard & Poor's makes it easier to do business in the secondary securities market in most of the 50 states. Brokers who trade a listed stock do not have to have the company's financials on file before they do business. The single listing, "blue skies," gives them clear trading status.

But when a company has been suspended, the rules change. Brokers had better have the company's financials on hand before they utter a single quote to a curious investor. Why? So that investors can be sure that the broker handling the quote has all the information needed to decide whether the quote is based on accurate and current information. The "blue sky" rule is direct and inclusive:

As a means reasonably designed to prevent fraudulent, deceptive, or manipulative acts or practices, it shall be unlawful for a broker or dealer to publish any quotation for a security or, directly or indirectly, to submit any such quotation for publication, in any quotation medium (as defined in this section) unless such broker or dealer has in its records the documents and information required by this paragraph (for purposes of this section, "paragraph (a) information"), and, based upon a review of the paragraph (a) information together with any other documents and information required by paragraph (b) http://www.law.uc.edu/CCL/34ActRls/#b of this section, has a reasonable basis under the circumstances for believing that the paragraph (a) information is accurate in all material respects, and that the sources of the paragraph (a) information are reliable.

Market Makers

Market makers played leading roles in the 1990s. For the first half of the decade, they ran amok and eventually landed themselves in the midst of a Justice Department investigation and a class action lawsuit that cost more than $1 billion to settle.

So, who are these guys, and what are they doing with your money?

A market maker is someone who, literally, makes a market for a stock. Unlike an exchange, where stocks are traded auction-style on the exchange floor, or face-to-face among brokers or between specialists, most Nasdaq stocks and all bulletin board issues are traded via market makers. They are the specialists of the over-the-counter market. Their job is to maintain an orderly market in certain securities by standing ready to buy or sell round lots at publicly quoted prices.

Publicly is a key word here. One of the main ways market makers make money is on the spread—the difference between the bid and ask prices. Bid is the price a buyer is willing to pay. Ask is the price at which a shareholder is willing to sell.

The ongoing abuse was tamed somewhat (especially among high-profile stocks) following an investigation by the Justice Department and the class action lawsuits that followed. However, market makers still have tremendous power over smaller and more thinly traded issues. And some market makers stack the deck further by acting as chop shops.

In a chop shop, a broker/dealer gets shares cheap, usually from an insider or through a private placement, and then sells them on the open market at market prices.

The potential for profit is enormous. Say a broker gets 1 million shares at 50 cents apiece, when the stock is trading at a bid–ask of $2 to $3 on the bulletin board. If sold immediately, the minimum profit is $1.5 million. But suppose the broker holds onto the shares and pushes them to unsuspecting investors through a boiler room operation. By selling the shares after they have been pumped up to, say, $10 a share, the spread (or chop) is that much deeper.

And let's not forget about the stock promoters, who are often the sources of the cheap stock in the first place. A company looking for a price bump is far more likely to go to a promoter rather than to a broker. Not only is the initial connection easier to make, but putting a layer between the company and the actual illegal conduct can sometimes help deflect trouble.

There's more than one way of turning worthless paper into cash. A ton of money can be made by pushing chop stocks to the sucker list, and the profit potential in shorting these same stocks is also enormous.

Shorting is borrowing shares at a price you're pretty sure is inflated; you're betting the price will go down—a lot. Say you want to short Company X, so you sell short 100 (borrowed) shares at $10, or $1,000. What you're actually doing is borrowing those shares from your broker and promising to replace them at a later date. If the share price goes down to $5 and you can replace those 100 shares while paying only $500, then the difference is pure profit.

Translate these numbers to a much grander scale—tens of thousands, or even millions, of shares are being shorted—

and a very lucrative game is under way. Shorting for profit goes on all the time. But it's not supposed to. Only marginable stocks can be shorted, and, to qualify for margin trading, stocks must have a "degree of national investor interest, the depth and breadth of market, and the availability of information respecting the stock." There's one other caveat to short selling: Stocks can only be shorted when they're on an up tick, not when they're in decline.

The downside, at least financially, is that if an investor bets wrong and the price of the stock goes up, paying back the "borrowed" shares can create a loss rather than a profit. Shorting risks everything, and sometimes even more.

How can you avoid this risk if the only way to trade in thousands of stocks is through a market maker? Know the company you're dealing with. If the company sounds eerily like a founding father, or seems similar to a big-name financial firm, but is not quite in the same class, do some digging.

But be aware that dealing with one of the "name brand" firms isn't necessarily a guarantee for a square deal either.

The Justice Department's investigation, and the lawsuits that followed, involved most of the big names in the U.S. brokerage industry. Goldman Sachs; Dean Witter; Donaldson, Lufkin & Jenrette; Hambrecht & Quist; J.P. Morgan, and Kidder Peabody were among the more than 30 named defendants.

Market makers and the various brokerage houses they worked for were accused of conspiring for more than five years, beginning in May 1989, to "raise, fix and maintain, and did raise, fix and maintain at supra-competitive levels the 'spread.'"

According to a complaint filed in U.S. District Court for the Southern District of New York in January 1998, market makers refused to quote shares in "odd eighths" (⅛, ⅜, ⅞), and would only handle trades that came in on even eighths. This meant that instead of having a ⅛ spread, the spread doubled to 25—lucrative terms in an already lucrative game.

Doubling the spread is an especially cruel joke on investors. The spread should be narrow, because of the competitive nature of the market makers' setup. Instead of having only one place, or station, to go to trade—as investors and their brokers do when they are dealing with stocks on an exchange—the over-the-counter market has several market makers ready to make a trade. Theoretically, they should be competing by offering the best spread. Instead, according to the Justice Department, they were in cahoots with each other to make the most money.

Occasionally, according to court documents, a rogue or novice trader tried to narrow the spread but was quickly heckled into submission or escorted out the door:

> Novice traders learn quickly that if they want to keep their jobs on an o-t-c desk, they will do well not to beat the price of fellow marketmakers. "Breaking the spread," as it is called, just isn't done. One veteran, who tried on occasion to narrow an o-t-c spread, told *Forbes:* "I used to get phone calls from people; they'd scream, 'Don't break the spread! You're ruining it for everybody else!'" Another trader who tried something similar said: "My phone lights up like a Christmas tree. 'Whaddya doing in the stock? You're closing the spread. We don't play ball that way. Go back where you belong."
>
> According to the NASD, from May 1, 1989 to May 1993, "average spreads on the Nasdaq National Market increased by over 37%, during which time

average spreads on the New York and the American stock exchanges have held steady. A study concluded that spreads were reduced by more than 50% on average when securities moved from trading on Nasdaq to trading on an exchange."

After news of a study that highlighted the fat spreads in the over-the-counter market, and announcement of a federal investigation, the spreads on many of the higher profile OTC issues suddenly dropped by half—or by an eighth, to be more exact.

Plaintiffs' losses were estimated in the billions. When the case was settled in July 1999, the defendants agreed to pay $1.03 billion—before fees and expenses. They did so without admitting any wrongdoing. Investors were guaranteed nothing more than a check for $25.

Chapter

5

CYBERSCAMMING

Although the Internet has spawned thousands of newsgroups, Usenets, chat rooms, message boards, and countless other places for people to swap stories, the financial world seems to have settled into a handful of sites for taking the investing public's pulse, or just catching up on the latest tall tales, rumors, and maybe a rare hot tip.

Silicon Investor (a subsidiary of Go2Net Inc.), Raging Bull (gobbled up by AltaVista, a division of CMGI Inc.), and Yahoo! cover most of the territory in stock chat land, although Yahoo! dropped its penny stock boards several years ago. America Online, Motley Fool, and TheStreet.com have similar forums, but not quite the same following.

But there's still plenty of grist on any of these boards, and an untold amount of crossover goes on among flamers, scammers, and mild-mannered posters, all of whom would like to turn a quick buck. A few boards remain dedicated to smoking out scams.

Silicon Investor (SI), launched in August 1995, is the granddaddy of the Internet stock chat room. When it opened online, it had a little chat competition from AOL, Compuserve, and Prodigy—the main Internet Service Providers (ISPs) at the time. Since then, Compuserve has become part of AOL and Prodigy has been expanding into Latin America.

After five years, SI boasts 2 million unique visitors each month, more than 13. 6 million messages posted by mid-2000 (an average of 20,000 posts daily), and 250,000 registered users at $200 a pop.

Jill Munden, who is now SI's public relations manager, nurtured the site's message board medium while she was SI's Web master for more than three years.

Munden says SI users tend to be a little more sophisticated, or at least a little more serious about their mission, because SI is the only one of the big three message boards that charges a registration fee.

Munden has watched the market evolve from the rough-and-tumble days when Lucent and Cisco were considered rough riders. In today's landscape, those same stocks are practically blue chips in the tech market.

"The gold rush keeps moving to different sectors," Munden says, noting that investors are not only moving among different sectors, they're learning all kinds of new tricks. "People are now doing a lot of options trading, and two years ago they didn't even know what it was. Individual investors are taking more risks in hopes of higher returns."

The media have tagged along with the huge influx of people who use the Internet not only for investing, but for doing research and swapping stock tips. "The press is really looking to these message boards to get an idea of investor sentiment," Munden says.

And although any financial adviser—and many people who use just plain common sense—will warn against ever basing an investment decision on something found on an online message board, skeptics might find these sites useful.

Despite all the drivel and hype that get passed around in these cyber bull sessions, there are kernels of truth that can lead investors down paths of due diligence they might not otherwise have found. In several instances, the criminal records of people who are now touting or heading up new companies have been revealed. Because it's not necessarily business related, this information is not on file with the SEC or the NASD. Some people have done a lot of legwork and investors only need to verify the information, rather than starting from scratch and ferreting it out themselves.

Silicon Investor's ThreadTalk, a digest of what's been sizzling recently among SI members, is a good place to catch up. One thread is devoted to lawsuits against chat room residents. Another, entitled "All Clowns Must be Destroyed," is devoted to slamming the most unrealistic of investors. "Voltaire's Porch," is a haven for philosopher-poets who just happen to be addicted to the stock market.

Raging Bull features profiles of members who are nominated by their peers for a closer look at both their investing philosophies and their lifestyles. Visitors have to hunt for quirky threads. Many of them pop up on Raging Bull's bookmark pages, which highlight members' favorite members, the most active boards of the day, and the boards most frequently bookmarked by members.

Yahoo!, with its absence of chatter about stocks trading on the bulletin board, is a bit more orderly. Readers are offered sites geared toward a variety of financial professionals (accountants, bankers, brokers), along with an extensive index of boards devoted to stocks traded on the major exchanges.

There's no lack of humor. Postings among the most depressed, distressed, and outright bankrupt firms are often full of subtle wit. The not so subtle humor often appears in the form of screen names such as "Moronbaiter" or "Bald Man from Mars."

An April 13, 2000, posting on the Raging Bull message board for Uniprime Capital (OTC BB: UPCA) read: "This stock is going to be gold mine! I say Strong buy! Buy all you can. This is the next MSFT! IMHO OF COURSE."

The poster's name? Upcaloser—a takeoff on the company's ticker symbol and the poster's position in the stock.

A Freudian slip, a deliberate thumbing of the nose at the clueless who would base their investments on advice from a message board, or simply the lament of someone who had already been taken? The posting came almost a year after the SEC had suspended trading in the company, which had issued a series of press releases saying it had an exciting new treatment for AIDS.

Uniprime

http://www.sec.gov/enforce/tsusp/34-41638.htm

http://www.sec.gov/enforce/litigrel/lr16252.htm

Uniprime Capital Acceptance, Inc. got a lot of attention when it was suspended from trading in July 1999. If proven true, it was the classic scam on so many fronts, including the way it got busted.

Until almost the day the company's shares were suspended from trading, Uniprime was a car dealership operating out of Las Vegas, and it had plans to expand nationwide.

In mid-June 1999, Uniprime flashed a message around the Web telling the world that, besides selling wheels, it had found a cure for AIDS. Even worse, Uniprime's Web site urged investors to "buy" its stock. Not a prudent move; Uniprime was not a registered investor adviser.

Undoubtedly, the SEC would have spotted Uniprime as the hype surrounding its AIDS cure translated into wild trading volumes. (Nearly 10 million shares traded in the four days preceding Uniprime's July 22 suspension; a week earlier, daily trading volume was between 11,000 and 30,000 shares.) But as luck would have it, the SEC got a heads up from another arm of the enforcement world. An NASD official spied the "Buy UPCA!" spam while fixing breakfast for his toddler.

Like many of its investigations, when the SEC looked into Uniprime, it ultimately focused on one man. Alfred J. Flores claimed to have tested Plasma Plus (the supposed AIDS miracle treatment) on five patients in Spain in 1990. Or wait, was it 1995? The exact date was important not only for scientific reasons, but for forensic reasons as well. In 1990, the year when Mr. Flores claimed he tested patients in a clinic outside of Madrid, the U.S. criminal justice system actually had him locked up in Colorado on charges of conspiracy to commit murder. Flores was in jail from 1986 to 1992, when he was paroled. Flores, who claimed to be an immunologist in Uniprime's press releases, maintained his innocence.

Regardless of the year—1990 or 1995—it would be ludicrous to assume that a successful AIDS treatment could be kept under wraps for five years, let alone an entire decade. But the message boards had an answer for that, too.

Apparently, a vast conspiracy among government agencies, the medical community, and the pharmaceutical companies had kept this lifesaving breakthrough out of the public's hands until Uniprime boldly brought it to the forefront. And yes, there truly are people out there who seem to believe the company's tale, or at least are not embarrassed about putting their pen names to it on the message boards and other Internet sites.

Only a small fraction of people posting on message boards use their real names. Most come up with quirky or cryptic screen names. Or, like our friend UPCA loser on the raging bull message board on the Uniprime Capital board, some dabble in ambiguity.

Some of these chat jockeys have earned quite a following. Several have been followed right to the courthouse steps by the SEC. Others have earned a reputation on both sides of the Street for their tenacious pursuit of scams and an uncanny knack for exposing hustlers long before law enforcement can wend its way through the legal process and shut them down.

The matriarch of these self-styled scam busters is Janice Shell, an art historian and American expatriate living in Milan. Shell stirs up strong feelings on almost any side of the Internet investing table. She has been lauded by enforcers as a welcome pebble in the shoes of scam artists, vilified by those she has exposed, cherished by those she has rescued, and threatened by some who blame her for their losses.

Shell and other private citizens have also been sued—usually by companies that claim they've been defamed, but also by businesses that can't take a joke. On April 1, 1999 (April Fools' Day), Shell and two of her SI message board buddies sent out a press release heralding a company that was selling pieces of the Internet. Shell and her cohorts did it not only as a April Fools' spoof, but to draw attention to how even the flakiest premise would have credibility with some portion of the investing public. And they were right. More than 1,700 people were curious about how they could invest as much as $100,000 in "FBN Associates." But no money was ever collected, nor was FBN an actual company. Even the most obvious question—what does FBN stand for?—might have shooed most of them away. FBN stands for Fly-by-Night. But the joke turned sour after Business Wire, Inc. sued Shell and two others for using its service to broadcast the hoax. The suit was eventually dropped.

Some of the "bashers" have a pretty good track record. In 1999, the SEC halted four out of five stocks being tracked by an SI group on a thread entitled "One Big Scam."

The Medium Is the Message

Another company that gathered quite a following on the message boards was eConnect, which you'll recall from the tree trimmer's tout in Chapter 4. In less than two years, eConnect generated 130,000 messages on Raging Bull alone, and a more modest 10,000 posts on SI.

A glance at a snapshot of eConnect's trading history—share price and volume—between February 29 and March 27, 2000, gives an idea of how powerful, as communications media, the message boards and newswires can be.

With a handful of exceptions, eConnect had been trading below $1 on a couple million shares per day for most of 1999 and into 2000. In early January 2000, the price crept above $1 but never broke the $2 mark, and daily volume remained in the 1 to 5 million shares range. But on February 29, volume picked up dramatically; more than 16 million shares changed hands. The price almost doubled, closing at $2.50. During the next nine trading days, 127 million eConnect shares were traded, and the stock hit an all-time high of $21.88. But on March 13, before the SEC suspended trading for 10 days, fewer than 20,000 shares were exchanged. When eConnect resumed trading on March 27, more than 13 million shares were dumped on the market. The stock opened at $1 and hit a low of $0.38 before closing at $1.75.

Not surprisingly, the conspiracy theorists were busy. One suggested the SEC had been taken in by eConnect's bashers and was issuing its trading suspension based merely on what its investigators had read online. Another tossed out the idea that attorneys filing class action lawsuits against eConnect had in some way orchestrated the trading halt. eConnect blamed the trading frenzy on promotions that it had nothing to do with.

For all of the ill attributed to the message boards, many agree that they have a positive side, and some would claim that the boards have actually helped investors, especially those who have shunned traditional brokers.

"It's been a real revolution in how people are getting their investing advice, and sharing it, and not listening to brokers," says David Zgodzinski, author of Silicon Investor's "ThreadTalk" and a former stockbroker.

A majority of SI's members, Zgodzinski is convinced, are employed in the world of technology, including many engineers. Their understanding of the technology, not to mention the inner workings of some of the top companies, is invaluable and available only online.

"I'll wager there isn't an investment information officer at a public company who doesn't scout the boards for that company," Zgodzinski says. "And soon, they'll be contributing. They'll realize this is what shareholders want. It will be the kind of dialogue they would have with analysts on a regular basis because they know how important it is to cultivate those kinds of relationships.

"Companies will be treating the message boards as a legitimate source for getting information out to shareholders. It's not just a Utopian dream; it's unavoidable. And once that develops, message boards become more important than other media—more important than television or newspapers. They're all going to come to the board because the board is going to be the center of information about that company.

"The boards are going to become the heart of investment information for the future."

And a lot of what ends up on the message boards gets started in what is, for the most part, a very legitimate means of communication: press releases. For a fee, any company—or any individual, for that matter—can get an account with either PR Newswire or Business Wire, which disseminate press releases to hundreds of news services and Internet sites around the world.

The growing acceptance of message boards as a source of information has regulatory and industry officials concerned. At the moment, there are no specific rules governing message boards as they relate to trading information about securities, except that message posters must comply with SEC guidelines about truthfulness and disclosure.

But that might change. In 1999, it was recommended through an in-house decision, that the SEC should study the effect that message board postings have on the volatility of stock prices. (Anecdotal evidence showed there was a parallel.) It also was suggested that brokerages hosting online discussion forums should adopt practices that will prevent investor confusion. That issue is at the heart of the controversy over whether message boards should be regulated by the SEC, the NASD, or anyone else. Readers may find it difficult to decipher what's accurate, what's purely "noise," and what's a flat-out lie.

There is no mad rush to regulate—at the moment. Incidents such as the March 1999 posting on a PairGain Technologies message board might change that. A PairGain employee posted a message on a Yahoo! finance board stating that PairGain would soon be bought out by an Israeli company. The hoax went even further; readers were linked to a fake Bloomberg News Service site that "reported" the acquisition. This "news" fueled heavy trading in PairGain shares, which rose by almost one-third before the truth was discovered. The stock then dropped 20 percent.

PairGain survived the hoax intact and was acquired by ADC Telecommunications, Inc. in June 2000. The hoaxster pleaded guilty to two felony counts of securities fraud and served five months under home detention before beginning five years on probation. He will also pay $93,000 in restitution.

It has been suggested that anyone who wants to post information about a company should be required to register under his or her real name, rather than anonymously. But this requirement might run into legal problems. The U.S. Supreme Court has already ruled that the First Amendment's right to free speech includes the right to remain anonymous, at least in the context of political speech.

Government enforcement officials are always surfing the Web in search of scams, and tapping into the seedy underworld of stock hustlers. Rarely, however, does anyone know that they're there.

Home computers, camouflaged computers, and e-mail accounts, and a host of other stealth options keep their identity concealed. Some call it entrapment, but the enforcement folks simply call it undercover work.

When they do pull off the mask, it almost always means trouble.

"THIS IS AN OFFICIAL ANNOUNCEMENT FROM THE U.S. SECURITIES & EXCHANGE COMMISSION" is the last thing touts and investors want to see in the subject heading on their favorite chat site. And John Reed Stark is not a name you want to see as the author.

Chapter

6

KNOWLEDGE IS POWER

It's not all bad. The Internet presents tremendous opportunity for prudent investors who know how to analyze investment opportunities. Here are a few pointers on the right way to invest—from research to trading.

93

Arguably, the Internet was the twentieth century's single most important advancement for empowering individual investors. Only a few years ago, most investors relied on full-service stockbrokers and professional portfolio managers (mostly through mutual funds) to make major decisions and to handle the day-to-day management of their investments. Access to current and detailed investment research was expensive and cumbersome. Access to basic investment information, such as current or real-time stock quotes, was nearly nonexistent.

Most investors settled for the day-old stock prices published in the business section of their daily newspapers. Account statements came in the snail mail once a month so investors could see how much their portfolio was worth a week ago.

The Internet has democratized the stock market and leveled the playing field for all investors, regardless of their net worth. Coupled with a strong economy and an enduring bull market, the Internet has transformed the art of investing. Formerly the exclusive realm of very wealthy individuals and professional traders, investing has become a staple of American popular culture.

Along with this migration of the masses to the stock market, there has been a surge in financial service providers, information and research services, media sources, and, of course, scam artists. To make responsible and profitable investment decisions, today's investors must be able to distinguish among them.

Besides knowing how to avoid a bogus stock tip or a scam, it's important to know where to go and how to use the Internet for personal investing needs.

Ideas

The financial Internet is loaded with ideas for investors. Mega sites like CBS Marketwatch and The Street.com offer dozens of articles and features that deliver opinions and analyses of the latest hot stocks and sectors. Some investors frequent public message boards to find and share ideas and opinions with their peers. Brokerage houses and independent research firms offer thousands of analysts' reports.

Off-line, there's just as much information, mostly from the financial media: magazines, newsletters, and the wildly popular CNBC television network. Interspersed with these sources are dozens of bogus or fraudulent sources that try to pass themselves off as unbiased research or expert opinions but are in reality stock promoters who may have an agenda contrary to the interests of potential shareholders.

Any number of stock-picking services can be tapped, on- and off-line. Some claim to use sophisticated computer formulas. Stock Detective puts little credence in stock-picking services. According to watchdog and author Mark Hulbert, even the most respected and experienced stock pickers seldom beat the market in the long run.

Research

Research has been the cornerstone of institutional investors for ages. Before the Internet, most of the truly comprehensive research was beyond the reach of most individual investors. Today, dozens of Web sites offer a plethora of both fundamental and technical research information. From quotes to charts, news, analysts' opinions, earnings estimates, financial statements, and historical performance, research drives investors as much as all the brokers, gurus, and stock tipsters in the world. More than anything else, research is a personal responsibility.

Research is usually divided into two broad categories: (1) technical and (2) fundamental.

Technical research involves analysis of the price and the trading volume history of a stock. Charts are at the heart of technical analysis. They display price and volume information, reveal patterns, and potentially forecast future changes.

Many professional money managers, traders, and investors swear by technical analysis and use very little other information to make their trading decisions. However, most investors, except the experienced (and rarely successful) day traders, should not rely on technical analysis alone. Long-term investing means choosing stocks that will live up to or exceed the expectations of most investors regarding fundamental growth and accomplishments such as increasing sales, market share, earnings, and so on.

But technical analysis and charting remain useful tools for ordinary investors and armchair Stock Detectives alike. The recent historical price and volume information of a stock are especially useful in efforts to determine the emotional characteristics of a stock, to pinpoint entry and exits, and to ferret out potential fraudulent or manipulated stocks.

Many stocks that become the subjects of hype or manipulation appear to undergo dramatic changes in their charts. They often are marked by sudden increases in price as well as trading volume. Typically, sharp price spikes on unusually high volume will be followed by declining prices and ebbing volume. This is a classic signature of most pump 'n' dump schemes. The NASD OTC Bulletin Board site (www.otcbb.com) provides a daily "most active" list of OTCBB stocks, and a number of Web sites provide technical stock screeners that can help in locating some of these issues.

Fundamental research covers a wide body of developments and sources of information. Essentially, fundamental research is the study of the tangible characteristics of the company underlying the stock: the company's finances, the market for its goods and services, the profile of its managers and large shareholders, and the opinions of its investors and analysts. Individuals wishing to conduct their own fundamental research can use a number of Internet sites and features to study thousands of widely followed stocks, and to research some more thinly traded and lesser known issues.

The popularity of a stock and the amount of research available on it pretty much go hand-in-hand. A search for information about some of the largest blue-chip and technology stocks—IBM, Microsoft, and Boeing, for example—will yield countless profiles, analysts' reports, earnings estimates, and, of course, the company's own financial statements and news releases. A search for an OTC or smaller Nasdaq or New York Stock Exchange (NYSE) issue will yield far fewer results.

News

Without much doubt, news drives markets and stock prices. If U.S. Federal Reserve Chairman Alan Greenspan says he's raising interest rates, stocks may plummet. The Justice Department says it wants to break up Microsoft, and competitors' shares take off. Earnings announcements from widely followed stocks are headlines in the financial press, on television, and on the Internet.

Mergers, acquisitions, bankruptcies, or any other news that affects the perception of the value of a public company is likely to affect the value of its shares.

Most financial sites, online brokers, and Internet portals offer financial news and company press releases sorted by stock symbols. This is an extremely convenient resource for self-directed investors. And the fact that so much news is available so quickly, and most of it is free on the Internet, has empowered investors as much as online trading and quotes.

Almost anywhere on the Internet, company news or press releases originate principally from two types of news sources: discretionary and nondiscretionary news wires. Discretionary news wires include Dow Jones, Reuters, Associated Press (AP), United Press International (UPI), and so on. These services receive news releases from companies and decide which ones to send to their customers. The stories are edited at the service's discretion. Company news and press releases on nondiscretionary wire services are dominated by Business Wire and PR Newswire. These and similar services are conduits for whatever a company has to say. They generally do not edit content, they just pass it along. As a result, recipients have no assurance that the information they are reading is objective and not pure promotion.

Trading

Thanks to the Internet, trading stocks has never been better. Today's average investor can do it cheaply and more efficiently than ever before. Dozens of online brokerage firms offer fast, inexpensive trading services complete with real-time quotes, research tools, up-to-the-minute account statements, bill paying, and many other services.

Investors are no longer bound to the confines of their desktop or cubicle. Technology marches on, and investors can now continue to annoy their friends and families with their trading addictions anywhere they go. Most of the leading on-line brokers are now offering wireless trading if the investor has an Internet-compatible wireless phone or a personal data device such as a PalmPilot.

Trading stocks is easy, but it's also perilous for inexperienced investors. A few simple rules can help keep most investors out of trouble.

Day Trading

For starters, day trading—trading in and out of stocks, often on a daily basis, but sometimes weekly—simply does not work. Many other investors and experts say that investors can day-trade stocks and make money like professionals and market makers do. We say they're wrong. Day trade and you'll more than likely lose your shirt.

A report by the North American Securities Administrators Association in 1999 concluded that 70 percent of day traders lose money. And that's in a raging bull market!

In the book, *Day Traders,* Greg Millman says he knows of several day traders who have attempted suicide, and many others who lost their life savings. Millman also warns investors who think they want to day trade that unscrupulous day-trading firms, powerful market makers and personal inexperience combine to make day trading a very risky vocation that is suitable for very few investors.

If you think you want to be a day trader, put down this book and look somewhere else for guidance.

Trading Online—Getting Started

Investing for medium- and longer-term gains is considered prudent and has become a do-it-yourself proposition through the Internet. The first step: Choose an online broker.

Most online brokers require stock trading fees (once known as commissions) ranging from a low of about $8 a trade to around $35 a trade. The 1999 SEC report showed a dramatic drop in average commissions since online trading has taken hold. Among the top 10 online brokerage firms, the average commission in 1996 was $52.89. Three years later, that number had plummeted by almost 75 percent to $15.75.

Traditional brokers are following investors online, to avoid losing customers to technology. The growth in online trading isn't confined to new investors, although they certainly have a strong presence. Mutual fund investors who have decided to dabble in stocks, and employees who are taking control of their retirement funds are other significant sources of growth. Investors who are moving away from a full-service broker, and some who maintain a traditional, full-service account while opening an online account with a discount broker round out the lot.

There are more than 100 brokers online, and their costs and services vary widely. A good rule of thumb is that you may get what you pay for—the deeper the trading discount, the fewer ancillary services you are likely to receive. Before you pick a broker, don't just compare price. Consider the other services offered and the quality of service you expect. If you want 24-hour live broker or customer service telephone support, or free unlimited real-time stock quotes, or check writing, bill paying, a debit card, a mutual fund marketplace, and so on, you'll probably end up closer to the higher end of the online and discount brokers. The opposite is true for the lower end, where low trading costs are emphasized over service and features.

Be sure to read the fine print. Brokers like to advertise their least expensive rates but typically offer those rates only in connection with certain types of trades. For example: E*Trade charges $14.95 for market orders for NYSE and AMEX listed securities and $19.95 for all Nasdaq orders and for limit orders on the exchanges. Deep discounter Brown and Company charges as little as $5 for market orders, but twice as much for limit orders.

Fees will also vary for frequent traders, broker assisted trades, or for large-share volume trades. Brown and company jumps from $5 to $65 if you trade 5,000 shares or more. E*Trade charges as little as $4.95 for investors who make 75 or more trades per quarter, and Ameritrade charges a $10 premium for broker assistance.

Most brokerages charge different fees for different types of trades. Market orders on OTC and Nasdaq shares are often the cheapest, and broker-assisted trades are the most expensive. Some firms offer discounts to active traders or those with large accounts.

One important feature to consider when choosing an online broker is whether he or she (or the firm) will offer support and trading assistance. What will you do if your computer, ISP, or online brokerage has technical problems and you can't place a trade? You'll probably want a live operator.

It's definitely worth your while to compare a few leading online brokerages before opening an account. Visit a few resources for broker comparison and research online. The best one is Gomez.com (http://gomez.com), a Massachusetts-based consulting firm. Also check out SmartMoney.com (http://smartmoney.com), a site that rates online and full-service brokers.

The Art of the Trade

Before you trade, you need to know *how* to trade. Trading online may be fairly simple, but it's critical that you understand the basic types of orders and a few things about the reality and risks of order execution, or you could be very sorry.

Unfortunately, too many online investors, unaware of the different order types, often lose money. Each type has its own advantages and disadvantages, and each is usually appropriate for a different circumstance.

Market Order

This is the most common order entered. A market order instructs a broker to buy or sell a stock at "the market," regardless of the price of the stock.

Market orders typically come with the lowest commissions, but they also carry the greatest risk to your portfolio because you have no control over the buy or sell price you'll receive after the order is entered.

For example, place a market order to buy Microsoft when it's offered at 70 and you could get a confirmation from your broker that you paid 70½, 71, or more, if the stock's price is moving fast. The same risk applies for selling shares.

During a recent dot-com mania, many Internet IPOs experienced wild price swings shortly after entering the market. When Palm, Inc. went public in March 2000, its shares, which were sold in its IPO at $38, opened up on the first day of trading at $150, shot up to $165, and, less than seven hours later, closed at $95 a share. Two months later, the stock was trading for as little as $20 a share.

Such volatility is usually attributed to inexperienced investors' placing market orders on the first day of trading in a stock. In the absence of an offsetting number of sell orders, they momentarily drive the price of the stock to unusual heights. Needless to say, most investors buying shares at the market on those occasions watch share prices fall just as quickly as those markets reach equilibrium.

In shares of thinly traded or low-priced stocks, market orders tend to be even less advantageous. Market makers in these stocks exercise unusual control over their trades and will not hesitate to take advantage of a market order for their gain, at your expense.

But market orders do have a place. They are best used in trading shares of large capitalization stocks or stocks that trade very actively within fairly stable ranges. A good example is shares of large industrial or blue-chip companies such as IBM, Cisco, or Exxon. These stocks may experience occasional volatility, but their usual trading patterns are characterized by large daily volume and small price swings. Market orders in stocks like these can avoid trading commissions and ensure prompt execution.

Limit Order

A limit order specifies a buy or sell price. A broker who is given a limit order has an obligation to execute the trade (1) at the price specified; (2) at a price better than the one specified;

or (3) not at all if there are not sufficient shares for sale or purchase at the specified price.

Limit orders protect your price but they risk your order's not being executed. Place a limit order on a fast falling or rising stock and, by the time your broker gets to trade it, the price may have moved beyond your "limit" and caused you to miss an opportunity.

Stop Order

A stop order is two orders in one. It provides a trigger price for a market order or a limit order.

The two types of stop orders are: stop loss and stop limit.

A stop loss order will trigger a market order to sell when the price of the stock falls to a specified or stop price. The actual execution price may be different—even less—if the price of the stock is falling quickly. A stop limit order is used to buy or sell stock when a price passes through the stop price but is under a limit order specifying a particular price.

Stop loss orders are excellent means of protecting a position against further loss when a stock price declines and you are not available to direct an order. If you go on vacation, you may want to place a few of these under stocks that you will want to sell if they fall below a designated price. Stop limits have similar appeal but they lack the guarantee of execution that the market orders have under stop loss.

Order Time Frame

When you provide order instructions to your online (or offline) broker, you will need to instruct him or her about how long to keep your order, pending its execution. There are only two types of time instruction: day orders and good-till-canceled (GTC) orders.

Order Execution Risks

Trading online is not a guarantee of accurate or timely trades. When you trade online, you take certain risks that could adversely impact your investment performance. Some of those risks are market risks. Others are directly related to the potential shortcomings of online trading.

One such risk is timely order execution. When you click your "place order" button on your computer, your order leaves your control for the moment and is in the hands of your electronic broker. Some orders may be executed very quickly—even within moments. Other orders may take several minutes or more, and you risk missing out on the price you saw on your screen when you decided to place the trade.

Another risk is technology. Online investors depend on reliable technology. Your computer, your broker's computers, the phone lines, Internet routes, and other technological factors can conspire to lose your order or prevent you from communicating with your broker.

Margin

Margin is the practice of buying stocks with money borrowed from a broker. Most brokers allow investors to buy twice as much stock as they have cash on hand, or 50 percent more than the value of the stocks in their account. Either way, the broker charges interest on the amount borrowed. Margin can leverage or increase profits in a rising market.

Example 1. Two investors have $25,000 each. The first investor purchases 1,000 shares of XYZ at $25 a share. On the same day, another investor purchases 2,000 shares of XYZ for $25 a share, after borrowing another $25,000 "on margin." A year later, both investors sell all their shares of XYZ for $50 a share. The first investor now has $50,000, or a 100 percent gain. The second investor, however, sold 2,000 shares for $100,000, repaid $27,000 ($25,000 plus 8 percent interest) borrowed on margin, and netted $73,000 (a 192 percent gain) on the same $25,000 original investment.

But with reward comes risk. Margin increases investors' buying power and leverages their profit potential. But at the same time, it increases the potential for loss. In a falling market, the second investor is going to lose money at twice the rate of the first investor. And brokerage firms are not about to take more risk than they can afford. If a stock drops too far, the investor will be asked to put up more cash or stock as collateral, or must risk being "bought in." When that happens, a lot of money—all of it, in fact—can be lost.

Example 2. The two investors described above see XYZ fall to $15 a share a year later. Each sells all his XYZ stock. The first investor sells 1,000 shares for $15 a share, leaving him with $15,000. He suffers a $10,000 loss from his original $25,000 investment. The second investor sells all his stock—2,000 shares for $15 a share—but is left holding only $3,000. From the $30,000 proceeds of his sale, he had to pay back $27,000 in margin principal and interest. This investor lost nearly 90 percent while the first investor lost only 40 percent.

In bull markets, investors become confident and the use of margin increases. But bear markets and sharp corrections in bull markets are inevitable. Being in the wrong place at the wrong time on a margin is risky, so govern yourself accordingly.

Options

Options are part of what are often referred to as "derivatives." Derivatives are securities that do not represent debt or ownership in a particular corporation or investment fund. Instead, they are based on the price of a certain stock, index, or other security. That security is referred to as the *underlying security*. Options are, perhaps, the stock market's version of legalized gambling. They involve a complex array of orders, position types, and strategies. Some option strategies are conservative and can actually be used to reduce or "hedge" the risk in a stock portfolio. Others are bought and sold purely for speculation.

There are two basic types of options: puts and calls. Puts increase in price when the price of the underlying security decreases. Calls increase in price when the price of an underlying security increases.

Because options are risky, brokerage firms must grant special authorization before a client can trade them. Generally, there is no special prerequisite. The client simply completes a standard form attesting to his or her knowledge of options and their risks. The broker is required to provide an options handbook that outlines and explains options strategies, types, and risks. But it's up to the client to read and understand it.

Options are for investors with advanced skills and a high tolerance for risk.

Several independent sites provide primers on options for novice investors, as well as information for seasoned investors. One of the best sites is OptionSource.com (www .optionsource.com), run by Schaeffer's Investment Research, a Cincinnati options-research firm. Click on the education tab, and this site will take you through a comprehensive on-line tutorial on the basics of options investing. You also can study more advanced options strategies and attend live cy-berseminars with options experts. The Options Industry Council (www.optionscentral.com), an industry trade group, provides access to educational material and an online sched-ule of free educational seminars across the country.

Short Selling

Perhaps the riskiest of all investment strategies, short selling offers unlimited risk for limited gain. In a nutshell, short sell-ing is the strategy of speculating on the fall in a stock's price for profit.

Short selling and margin trading have much in common. Brokers apply similar collateral rules to customers who sell short. Additionally, there are federal short selling regulations. One is that a stock must be considered marginable before it can be sold short. Eligible stocks are generally limited to shares of stocks trading on major exchanges and exceeding $5 in price.

Your broker won't let you sell short until you first con-vince him or her that you are a fool who can afford to part with lots of money, real fast.

Chapter

7

TOO LITTLE, TOO LATE

*Try as it may, the SEC is **too** short on people and funds to combat the growth of securities fraud—online and off. What is the future of enforcement, and how does an investor complain to the right people?*

Regulators know that, in the war on securities fraud, educating investors pays a higher dividend than trying to police all of cyberspace. "Investor protection—at its most basic and effective level—starts with the investor," SEC Chairman Arthur Levitt said in a statement in January 1999.

When John Reed Stark, chief of the SEC's Internet Enforcement Division, posts a trading suspension notice on message boards around the online investment community, it can be the death knell for a company—even one that manages to start trading again after the suspension is lifted.

None of the 27 companies that have had their trading suspended by the SEC since January 1999 has reestablished trading on the OTC bulletin board, although at least one is actively trading on the Vancouver Stock Exchange and a number are active in the pink sheets.

A trading suspension might be the beginning of the end for a company's publicly traded shares, but it's often just a rest stop in the SEC's investigative process. "Suspending trading is really just to take a breath," says Stark, who has been focusing on Internet fraud since 1994. The Internet has become almost as valuable a tool to law enforcement as it has for scam artists.

And the SEC isn't the only regulatory or law enforcement agency that has gone online to combat securities fraud.

The National Association of Securities Dealers Regulation division (NASDR) is no stranger to the medium. Its investigators use it regularly—and not so regularly. One NASD employee spotted a scam while feeding his child breakfast.

Before the day was out, trading in Uniprime Capital Acceptance had been halted.

State agencies also use the Web as a tool. At California's Department of Corporations, investigators often lurk on message boards or pose as investors.

"There's something fabulous about getting ourselves on junk mailing lists and shutting them down before they can do any damage," said the California Department of Corporations' Marc Crandall. Crandall led the prosecution of one of California's most ludicrous Internet investing schemes. By various means—spam, message boards—investors were drawn to a Web site that gave them the opportunity to invest in a time machine. This was the theory the company proffered: Their premise of a time machine would attract so much publicity that, when one was actually invented in the future, those people would come back (via time travel?) and give them the technology to build one. Unfortunately, at least a few people actually invested in this ruse before California shut the venture down.

But cases like these raise issues of free speech and jurisdictional concerns that are outside the realm of securities fraud. Crandall found the posting about the time machine on Yahoo!'s message boards. Like its sister forum sites, Yahoo! takes no responsibility for what gets posted there; however, it will delete a posting under some conditions. Some would argue that postings like those associated with the time machine scam, and similar shenanigans, lay the groundwork for government agencies to do more than monitor these sessions, and that kind of posting should be banned.

Well, in a sense, it is already banned. It's illegal to make false and misleading statements concerning an investment opportunity. But a prohibition usually means that (1) someone with the proper authority has to know about the posting, and (2) an investigation into whether the statement is actually false and misleading must be undertaken. By the time either or both of those responses happen, it could be too late for many investors. On the other hand, if people would simply know enough to laugh when they see "time machine" and "investment opportunity" in the same paragraph, perhaps there would be no talk of censorship.

As for jurisdictional issues, it's still not clear how U.S. authorities will be able to pursue scam artists who are operating outside U.S. borders, even if their victims are U.S. citizens.

As the world shrinks to the size of a computer screen, the need for cooperation will grow.

States generally prosecute fraud that originates within their borders, and some will also warn investors about specific situations discovered outside the state regulators' jurisdiction. Ohio, for example, lists specific online securities offerings that investors are cautioned to avoid. Going a step further, investors are asked to contact the Ohio Department of Commerce's Securities Division if they are solicited for investment in any of the listed companies.

If you're surfing for securities regulators in a variety of states, it can take a little getting used to. For whatever reason, there is no uniform assignment within state governments in all 50 states. For example, in California, securities regulation falls to the Department of Corporations; in Ohio, it's a function of the Department of Commerce.

The SEC's in-house intranet has also developed into a resource for the Commission's enforcement agents. It includes a tool box and guidelines for sniffing out scams, as well as a watch list of companies that SEC insiders consider dangerously close to the line. For obvious reasons, the SEC's intranet is off limits to outsiders. But a good chunk of the SEC's MO is available to investors through its Web site and its extensive list of publications detailing almost every aspect of fraud and how to avoid it.

And the SEC needs all of the do-it-yourselfers it can get in the due diligence and common sense department.

The SEC's $361 million budget in 2000 reflected more than a 100 percent increase compared to the 1990 funding. Still, it has not allowed the SEC to keep pace with the growth of fraud. The SEC receives between 300 and 400 complaints *each day*—more than double the number coming in just three years ago. And, despite the explosion of the bull market and the stampede of investors into the market, the SEC's staff has grown by a paltry 36 percent since 1990.

Future budget increases are also in doubt. During the early rounds of budget talks for fiscal 2001, the House Appropriations Committee approved only half of the 12 percent increase the SEC had requested. That would have taken its funding to $422.8 million. Most of the requested increase was earmarked for additional staff to work on Internet-related fraud cases, and for raises for lawyers and accountants already on board.

Stark said turnover is high at the SEC, primarily because government pay rarely is competitive with the salaries professionals can make in the private sector, especially during such robust economic times.

"You have a problem with turnover when the market pays two or three times what we do," Stark said. He added that SEC attorneys work on a pay scale that is below that of other government attorneys. And turnover doesn't affect only caseloads. With the Internet presenting an increasingly tangled web of characters and opportunities, the learning curve is getting much steeper—and much faster. "It would just be nice to be able to retain some people with some institutional knowledge," Stark said.

A couple of months after the SEC's Office of Internet Enforcement was formally established, stock promoters got notice that the Commission was gearing up for battle. In late October 1998, the SEC named 44 individuals and companies in its first-ever nationwide sweep against Internet fraud. Of those charged, more than three-fourths have settled with the SEC, while the others remain in litigation. Most, in fact, had a settlement offer ready when they were charged, according to SEC documents. All those who settled did so without admitting or denying the allegations.

SEC offices in Atlanta, Boston, Chicago, Denver, Fort Worth, Los Angeles, Miami, New York, Philadelphia, Salt Lake City, and Washington, DC, all took part in the crackdown. Targets of the bust included Internet junk mail (spam), newsletters, Web sites, and message board activity. The SEC charges focused on violations of the antifraud and antitouting provisions of the securities laws. The defendants were accused of touting more than 230 companies (mostly penny stocks) by "lying about the companies; lying about their own independence from the companies; and/or failing to disclose adequately the nature, source, and amount of compensation paid by the companies."

All told, those picked up in the sweep had taken in more than $6.3 million in cash and at least 2 million cheap shares of the stocks they were touting. The cash value of the shares could have been astronomical, depending on when they were sold. According to the SEC, a lot of them were sold shortly after the hype began, when the hucksters scalped their shares at a huge profit.

The SEC and the NASD might get the most ink, and break the most news; but there are plenty of investigative agencies outside the Beltway.

Each state has its own version of securities regulation (see Appendix A) although few share a common name for the office. The North American Securities Administrators Association (NASAA) is part of the regulatory and investigative mix as well. Investors today, especially the breed of investors who operate strictly on Internet time, think of the SEC as the granddaddy of regulation, but the NASAA (set up in 1919) predates the SEC by more than a decade. State securities regulations were modeled after a 1911 Kansas law known as "blue sky." According to NASAA, the term referred to "speculative schemes that, in the words of a judge of the period, had no more substance than so many feet of 'blue sky.'"

Since the SEC was established in 1934, state and federal regulators have sought different routes to the same goal: investor protection. The SEC's sweeps might get the most national press (when such things get any press at all), but state regulators are 50 times as busy, often going after smaller crooks who might slip through the SEC's wider nets.

And because each state is pretty much focused within its own borders, trouble is more likely to be spotted before it goes national, although the speed the Internet affords hustlers makes catching them more of a challenge. The Internet also can tangle jurisdictional guidelines. Just because something is illegal in Illinois, or in the entire United States, it doesn't mean it's against the law somewhere else. Increasingly, U.S. securities regulators are faced with dubious schemes that are coming from Europe, the Middle East, and that long-time haven for con artists, the Caribbean.

By the time Stark's moniker pops up on the message boards, it's usually too late for all but a handful of investors to bail out gracefully, or with any kind of profit—except for the shorts, of course. One of the most frustrating things investors face is the SEC's refusal to confirm or deny whether it is investigating a particular firm or individual. But there are good reasons for the SEC's silence. Besides making it easier to spy on people because they don't know the SEC is looking, just the mere thought of an SEC investigation could have harsh effects on a company's stock, regardless of whether the SEC ever finds evidence of wrongdoing.

If the SEC finds enough reason to bring an enforcement action against a company or individual, investors still might have to pursue restitution on their own. Although almost all enforcement actions brought by the SEC call for some kind of restitution or disgorgement, only a small fraction of those accused of fraud ever pay up. For the most part, the SEC is content to get these people to agree to stop violating securities laws; it doesn't have the resources or the reason to pursue those who "demonstrate an inability to pay." That's legalese for "I've stashed all of the money offshore and you can't touch it."

How to Complain to the Right People

Where do you turn for help? That usually depends on who you believe has done you wrong. A brokerage or registered representative? Contact NASD. A company or its officers? Notify the SEC. Your state securities regulator should also be notified in either case.

Before you go running to state or federal officials, try working things out with the locals, the people who are handling your money—or were until they ticked you off. If your broker is unresponsive, ask to talk to the branch manager. If that gets you nowhere, move up to the district manager before calling headquarters and asking for someone who not only controls the company, but also can write pink slips with impunity.

When things just don't work out, you don't have to give up. There are a number of avenues through which investors can pursue complaints against their investment advisers—whether they're brokers or financial planners, individual companies, or people who run them.

Most people start with the SEC, which has streamlined its complaint process and made it readily accessible to anyone with a computer or simply a telephone. The Web address is http://www.sec.gov/consumer/jcompla.htm. Appendix C gives contact information for the twelve SEC offices across the country.

Because the SEC gets so many complaints (between 300 and 400 daily), your first and quickest option will be to surf the SEC's site for an answer to your problem. The site has a pretty extensive list of common complaints, many of which can often be solved by the investor with a couple of phone calls.

Before you sign on with a broker, make sure you run his or her name—and the name of the firm—through the NASDR at http://pdpi.nasdr.com/pdpi/disclaimer_frame.htm, which keeps a database of all registered agents and all brokerage houses. Checking the Central Registration Depository (CRD) library can really short-circuit problems up front. A broker's CRD file will tell you, among other things, where he or she has worked, the states in which he or she is licensed to sell securities, and his or her disciplinary record—if there is one. The same information is available for the brokerage firms.

In most cases, if you have a problem with a broker, you may be limited in what you can do. Most brokerage contracts contain clauses that try to eliminate a client's right to sue the firm or an individual broker. The validity of these clauses has already been challenged and was upheld by the U.S. Supreme Court in *Shearson v. McMahon,* a 1987 decision.

If there is a complaint, these same contracts usually herd investors toward arbitration. This isn't necessarily a bad thing, although the cost of filing for arbitration is no longer dirt cheap. Fees increased, on average, by almost half in 1997; they now range from $25 to $600, depending on the amount of the claim. There is also a hearing deposit, again based on the amount of the claim. The deposit starts at $25 and tops out at $1,200 for a three-member panel that hears claims of more than $5 million.

Years may pass before you actually get to the table, so another forum for resolving complaints has been gaining in popularity: mediation. Although it's similar to arbitration in that objective third parties hear the dispute, mediation is generally faster and cheaper than the binding word of an arbitrator. If mediation settles the dispute, fine. But it's not the last word. If either side is unhappy with the proposed settlement, the dispute can be moved back to the arbitration docket, or, in some cases, brought into the court system. Getting either side to step forward and suggest mediation isn't always easy; the other party may consider it a sign of weakness. Brokers are especially leery of mediation because even a mediation settlement in their favor remains part of the permanent record. If a dispute is settled through the arbitration process and the broker is cleared of wrongdoing, the complaint is removed from his or her file.

There's no question that (1) the opportunity for fraud has exploded with the bull market, and (2) complaints are increasing, but the two problems have not developed along parallel lines. A strong market can often mask fraud. So long as their portfolios keep growing, many investors are not likely to analyze their monthly statements. This benign indifference causes many people to miss signs of churning: unsuitable investments and unauthorized transactions. So long as their net worth keeps going up, they simply aren't concerned with how or why it's happening.

The *Shearson* decision may have roped most investors into either arbitration or mediation when they're unhappy with their broker, but investors seeking redress against a company they hold an interest in are still quite welcome on the courthouse steps.

From 1996 to mid-2000, more than 870 securities fraud class action lawsuits were filed against companies in federal courts, according to the Stanford Securities Class Action Clearinghouse (http://securities.stanford.edu), which is a service of the Robert Crown Law Library at Stanford University. The year 1998 was the busiest: 244 class actions were filed, compared to 114 in 1996. Litigation dropped off in 1999 to 216 filings, and 2000 is on a pace for about 200 complaints to be filed.

A class action may be filed on behalf of a handful of plaintiffs or thousands. The numbers don't matter so long as they all have the same complaint against the company involved. As the first step in the class action process, a judge determines whether there is, in fact, a class of people who have a legitimate complaint.

Class actions can sneak up on people who may be seeking damages on their own. Once a class is certified, members of the class must opt out of that proceeding if they wish to pursue their own claim independently. If they don't, they'll be bound by whatever settlement is reached in the class action suit.

The $1 billion Nasdaq price-fixing case (see Chapter 4) was a class action, as was the massive case brought against Prudential Securities Inc. in the 1980s, by investors who had lost more than $1 billion in limited partnerships, a rare exception to the arbitration-only rule that applies to most client–broker disputes.

A new breed of class action complaint began cropping up in the 1990s. It was based on the "efficient market" theory, which holds that the market prices all stocks efficiently, because it immediately reacts to information about a company and translates that information into the share price. If this is true, then withholding information is considered a form of stock price manipulation.

The regulatory arm of the National Association of Securities Dealers (NASDR) also is very active in policing the industry. In particular, the NASDR keeps tabs on brokers and brokerage firms. But it also works closely with the SEC and state regulators.

Usually, arbitration starts with the NASDR. It has six regional dispute-resolution offices, but hearings are held in dozens of cities within those regions. So, for example, if you live in Dallas or Omaha, both of which are under the Chicago office's jurisdiction, you don't have to get on a plane. Hearings are held in both of those cities, and in many more. Several regional stock exchanges—Boston, Pacific, Chicago, Cincinnati, and New York—also handle disputes.

There are limits on the disputes that can go to arbitration. If your issue is with a company you've invested in, or its officers, don't come crying to the NASDR. This venue is strictly for brokers, the firms they work for, and any misdeeds you believe either has committed. There's also a time limit (six years) on filing a complaint. So don't stew about your complaint. Collect your documents and fill out the necessary forms if you are unable to resolve the dispute with the brokerage house yourself.

Complaints that have already been filed as a class action frequently are not eligible for arbitration.

Even after starting the arbitration process, individuals can petition for the right to pursue their claim in court. It's up to the sponsoring organization (i.e., the NASDR or one of the regional stock exchanges) or the arbitrators to decide whether the complaint can move along in the court system. More often than not, the arbitrators and sponsors nix the courts and keep the case in arbitration.

At that point, many investors turn to mediation. Since the NASDR started offering mediation as a remedy in broker–client disputes, the number of investors choosing that route has doubled. More than 3,000 cases have gone to mediation since August 1995. The NASDR claims an 80 percent settlement rate, which means that more than 2,400 complaints avoided the lengthy, and more expensive, arbitration process.

Mediation is seen as such a sleek and effective way of resolving disputes, that the NASDR even puts the process "on sale." Once a year, typically in August, the agency reduces the cost of filing for mediation "to encourage more parties to explore mediation's benefits." What started out as a weeklong special has grown to a monthlong markdown.

Among investors' top three complaints are: (1) unsuitable recommendations, (2) unauthorized transactions, and (3) churning—excessive trading in an account that runs up commissions but adds little value to the client's portfolio. Ironically, churning is sometimes authorized by investors who don't realize what's going on. Their broker calls with a recommendation that sounds like a good thing, so they give the go-ahead. This becomes a problem when the broker calls too frequently (egged on by a previous green light) and the customer continues authorizing trades, perhaps in hopes of regaining something that was lost on the last hot tip.

The NASD issued its first suitability rule in 1939. It reads, in part, that brokers must have "reasonable grounds that any recommendation they make to a customer is suitable, based on what the customer has disclosed, if anything, about other security holdings, financial situation, and needs." Over the years, the rule has become a strong, affirmative directive. Brokers are instructed to not just make a "suitable recommendation," but to "make certain determinations before making any recommendation to a noninstitutional customer." They can't just run through a checklist and decide that Mrs. Jones is suitable for Company B. They must be able to prove that they understood why Mrs. Jones was suitable for Company B and how it fit into her long- and short-term financial goals.

The question of suitability is taking on new meaning through the Internet. One of the issues the SEC and other self-regulatory organizations are facing is: At what point is an on-line brokerage merely providing information, and at what point is it making a recommendation?

A

SECURITIES REGULATORS: NORTH AMERICA

United States

ALABAMA

Securities Commission
770 Washington Avenue, Suite 570
Montgomery, Alabama 36130-4700
FedEx Zip: 36104
334/242-2984 or 800/222-1253
334/242-0240 (fax)
alseccom@dsmd.dsmd.state.al.us
• Joseph P. Borg, Esq.
  Director
  334/242-2386
  jborg@asc.state.al.us

Source: North American Securities Administrators Association. http://nasaa.org.
Includes United States, Puerto Rico, Canada, and Mexico.

ALASKA

Department of Community and Economic Development
Division of Banking, Securities, and Corporations
150 Third Street, Room 217
P.O. Box 110807
Juneau, Alaska 99811-0807
907/465-2521
907/465-2549 (fax)
http://www.dced.state.ak.us/bsc.htm
• Franklin Terry Elder
  Director of Banking, Securities, and Corporations Division
  terry_elder@dced.state.ak.us

ARIZONA

Corporation Commission
1300 West Washington, Third Floor
Phoenix, Arizona 85007
602/542-4242
602/594-7470 (fax)
accsec@ccsd.cc.state.az.us (e-mail)
www.cc.state.az.us
• W. Mark Sendrow
  Director of Securities
  602/542-0643
  602/594-7430 (fax)
  wms@ccsd.cc.state.az.us

ARKANSAS

Securities Department
Heritage West Building, Room 300
201 East Markham
Little Rock, Arkansas 72201
501/324-9260
501/324-9268 (fax)
arsec@ccon.net (e-mail)
http://www.state.ar.us/arsec
• Mac Dodson
  Commissioner

CALIFORNIA

Department of Corporations
320 West 4th Street
Suite 750
Los Angeles, California 90013-1105
213/576-7643
213/576-7182 (fax)
http://www.corp.ca.gov/srd/security.htm
• G.W. ("Bill") McDonald
  Assistant Commissioner
  Enforcement Division
  213/576-7615
  213/576-7181
  bmcdonal@corp.ca.gov

COLORADO

Division of Securities
1580 Lincoln, Suite 420
Denver, Colorado 80203
303/894-2320
303/861-2126 (fax)
http://www.dora.state.co.us/securities
• Fred J. Joseph
  Commissioner
  Fred.Joseph@dora.state.co.us

CONNECTICUT

Department of Banking
260 Constitution Plaza
Hartford, Connecticut 06103-1800
860/240-8230
860/240-8295 (fax)
http://www.state.ct.us/dob
• Ralph A. Lambiase
  Director
  860/240-8231

DELAWARE

Division of Securities
Department of Justice
820 North French Street, 5th Floor
Carvel State Office Building
Wilmington, Delaware 19801
302/577-8424
302/577-6987 (fax)
http://www.state.de.us/securities
- James B. Ropp
  Securities Commissioner
  302/577-8925

DISTRICT OF COLUMBIA

The Department of Insurance and Securities Regulation
Securities Bureau
810 First Street NE, Suite 701
Washington, DC 20002
202/727-8000
202/535-1199 (fax)

FLORIDA

Office of Comptroller
Department of Banking
101 East Gaines Street
Plaza Level, The Capitol
Tallahassee, Florida 32399-0350
850/410-9805
850/681-2428 (fax)
- Don Saxon
  Director, Division of Securities and Finance
  850/410-9805
  850/410-9431 (fax)

GEORGIA

Office of the Secretary of State
Division of Securities and Business Regulation
Two Martin Luther King, Jr. Drive SE
802 West Tower
Atlanta, Georgia 30334
404/656-3920
404/651-6451 (fax)
http://www.sos.state.ga.us
- Robert D. Terry
  Division Director
  Assistant Commissioner of Securities
  bterry@sos.state.ga.us

HAWAII

Department of Commerce and Consumer Affairs
1010 Richards Street, 2nd Floor
Honolulu, Hawaii 96813
Mailing address: P.O. Box 40
Honolulu, Hawaii 96810
808/586-2744
808/586-2733 (fax)
http://www.hawaii.gov/icsd/lrb/ph_dcca.htm
• Ryan S. Ushijima
  Commissioner of Securities
  ryan_s_ushijima@dcca.state.hi.us

IDAHO

Department of Finance
Securities Bureau
700 West State Street, 2nd Floor
Boise, Idaho 83720
Mailing address: P.O. Box 83720
Boise, Idaho 83720-0031
208/332-8004
208/332-8099 (fax)
http://www.state.id.us./finance/dof.htm
• Marilyn T. Chastain
  Bureau Chief
  208/332-8004
  mchastai@fin.state.id.us

ILLINOIS

Office of the Secretary of State
Securities Department
17 North State Street, Suite 1100
Chicago, Illinois 60601
312/793-3384 or 800/628-7937
312/793-1202 (fax)

Springfield office:
520 South Second Street
Suite 200 Lincoln Tower
Springfield, Illinois 62701
217/782-2256
217/524-2172 (fax)
http://www.sos.state.il.us
• William L. Houlihan
   Chief Deputy Director
   312/793-3384
   bhoulih@ccgate.sos.il.us

INDIANA

Office of the Secretary of State
Securities Division
302 West Washington, Room E-111
Indianapolis, Indiana 46204
317/232-6681
317/233-3675 (fax)
http://www.state.in.us/sos/security
• Bradley W. Skolnik
   Securities Commissioner
   317/232-6690
   bskolnik@sos.state.in.us

IOWA

Insurance Division
Securities Bureau
340 E. Maple
Des Moines, Iowa 50319-0066
515/281-4441
515/281-3059 (fax)
515/281-6467 (alternative facsimile)
http://www.state.ia.us/government/com/ins/security/
security.htm
• Craig A. Goettsch
  Superintendent of Securities
  Craig.Goettsch@comm6.state.ia.us

KANSAS

Office of the Securities Commissioner
618 South Kansas Avenue, 2nd Floor
Topeka, Kansas 66603-3804
785/296-3307 or 800/232-9580
785/296-6872 (fax)
ksecom@cjnetworks.com
http://www.ink.org/public/ksecom
• David R. Brant
  Securities Commissioner
  dbrant@cjnetworks.com

Wichita office:
Office of the Securities Commissioner
230 E. William, Suite 7080
Wichita, Kansas 67202
316/337-6280
316/337-6282 (fax)
kscict@feist.com (e-mail)
• Merilyn Bowman
  Senior Examiner
  mbowman@feist.com

KENTUCKY

Department of Financial Institutions
1025 Capital Center Drive, Suite 200
Frankfort, Kentucky 40601
502/573-3390 or 800/223-2579
502/573-8787 (fax)
http://www.dfi.state.ky.us/security/Security.html
• Colleen Keefe
  Division of Securities
  colleen.keefe@mail.state.ky.us

LOUISIANA

Securities Commission
3445 North Causeway Boulevard, Suite 509
Metairie, LA 70002
504/846-6970
• Harry C. Stansbury
  Deputy Securities Commissioner

MAINE

Department of Professional and Financial Regulation
Securities Division
121 State House Station
Augusta, Maine 04333-0121
207/624-8551
207/624-8590 (fax)
* Christine A. Bruenn
  Securities Administrator
  christine.a.bruenn@state.me.us

MARYLAND

Office of the Attorney General
Division of Securities
200 Saint Paul Place, 20th Floor
Baltimore, Maryland 21202-2020
410/576-6360
410/576-6532 (fax)
securities@oag.state.md.us (e-mail)
http://www.oag.state.md.us
* Melanie Senter Lubin
  Securities Commissioner
  410/576-6365
  mlubin@oag.state.md.us

MASSACHUSETTS

Secretary of the Commonwealth
Securities Division
One Ashburton Place, Room 1701
Boston, Massachusetts 02108
617/727-3548
617/248-0177 (fax)
• Matthew Nestor
  Director
  matthew.nestor@sec.state.ma.us

MICHIGAN

Office of Financial and Insurance Services
6546 Mercantile Way
Lansing, Michigan 48909
Mailing address: P.O. Box 30701
Lansing, Michigan 48901-8201
517/241-6350
517/241-6356 (fax)
http://www.cis.state.mi.us
• Ronald C. Jones
  Director, Securities Division
  ronald.c.jones@state.mi.us

MINNESOTA

Department of Commerce
133 East Seventh Street
St. Paul, Minnesota 55101
651/296-4026
651/296-4328 (fax)
commerce@state.mn.us
http://www.commerce.state.mn.us
• Scott P. Borchert
   Director, Enforcement Division
   651/296-9431
   651/296-4328 (fax)
   scott.borchert@state.mn.us

MISSISSIPPI

Secretary of State's Office
Securities Division
202 North Congress Street, Suite 601
Jackson, Mississippi 39201
Mailing address: P.O. Box 136
Jackson, Mississippi 39205
601/359-6371
601/359-2663 (fax)
• Leslie Scott
   Assistant Secretary of State, Business Services
   lscott@sos.state.ms.us

MISSOURI

Office of the Secretary of State
600 West Main Street
Jefferson City, Missouri 65101
573/751-4136
573/526-3124 (fax)
http://mosl.sos.state.mo.us
• Douglas F. Wilburn
  Commissioner of Securities
  dwilburn@mail.sos.state.mo.us

MONTANA

Office of the State Auditor
Securities Department
840 Helena Avenue
Helena, Montana 59604
Mailing address: P.O. Box 4009
Helena, Montana 59604
406/444-2040
406/444-5558 (fax)
• Brenda K. Elias
  Deputy Securities Commissioner

NEBRASKA

Department of Banking and Finance
Bureau of Securities
1200 N Street, Suite 311
Lincoln, Nebraska 68508
Mailing address: P.O. Box 95006
Lincoln, Nebraska 68509-5006
402/471-3445
http://www.ndbf.org
- Jack E. Herstein
  Assistant Director
  jackh@bkg.state.ne.us

NEVADA

Secretary of State
Securities Division
555 E. Washington Avenue
5th Floor, Suite 5200
Las Vegas, Nevada 89101
702/486-2440
702/486-2452 (fax)
nvsec@govmail.state.nv.us (e-mail)
http://www.sos.state.nv.us
- Donald J. Reis
  Chief Deputy Secretary of State
  702/486-2440
  702/486-2452 (fax)

Reno office:
Office of the Secretary of State, Securities Division
1105 Terminal Way, Suite 211
Reno, Nevada 89502
775/688-1855
775/668-1858 (fax)

NEW HAMPSHIRE

Bureau of Securities Regulation
Department of State
State House, Annex—Room 317A
25 Capital Street
Concord, New Hampshire 03301
Mailing address: Room 204, State House
Concord, NH 03301-4989
603/271-1463
603/271-7933 (fax)
• Peter C. Hildreth
  Director of Securities Regulation
  philreth@sos.state.nh.us

NEW JERSEY

Department of Law and Public Safety
Bureau of Securities
153 Halsey Street, 6th Floor
Newark, New Jersey 07102
Mailing address:
P.O. Box 47029
Newark, New Jersey 07101
973/504-3600
973/504-3601 (fax)
* Franklin L. Widmann
  Chief, Bureau of Securities
  973/504-3610
  973/504-3639 (fax)

NEW MEXICO

Regulation and Licensing Department
Securities Division
725 St. Michaels Drive
Santa Fe, New Mexico 87505-7605
505/827-7140 (general information)
505/984-0617 (fax)
RLDSD@state.nm.us
* William Verant
  Acting Director

NEW YORK

Office of the Attorney General
Investor Protection Securities Bureau
120 Broadway, 23rd Floor
New York, New York 10271
212/416-8200
212/416-8816 (fax)
www.oag.state.ny.us
• Eric R. Dinallo
  Bureau Chief
  212/416-8989

NORTH CAROLINA

Department of the Secretary of State
Securities Division
300 North Salisbury Street, Suite 100
Raleigh, North Carolina 27603-5909
919/733-3924
919/821-0818 (fax)
http://www.secstate.state.nc.us
Mailing address:
North Carolina Securities Division
P.O. Box 29622
Raleigh, NC 27602-0525
• David S. Massey
  Deputy Securities Administrator
  dmassey@mail.secstate.state.nc.us

NORTH DAKOTA

Securities Commissioner
State Capitol, 5th Floor
600 E. Boulevard
Bismarck, North Dakota 58505-0510
701/328-2910
701/255-3113 (fax)
seccom@state.nd.us (e-mail)
• Syver Vinje
  Commissioner
  svinje@state.nd.us

OHIO

Division of Securities
77 South High Street, 22nd Floor
Columbus, Ohio 43215
614/644-7381
614/466-3316 (fax)
http://www.securities.state.oh.us
• Thomas E. Geyer
  Commissioner
  614/644-9530
  tom.geyer@com.state.oh.us

OKLAHOMA

Department of Securities
First National Center, Suite 860
120 N. Robinson
Oklahoma City, Oklahoma 73102
405/280-7700
405/280-7742 (fax)
http://www.securities.state.ok.us
- Irving L. Faught
  Administrator
  ilf@securities.state.ok.us

OREGON

Department of Consumer and Business Services
Division of Finance and Corporate Securities
350 Winter Street NE, Room 410
Salem, Oregon 97301-3881
503/378-4387
503/947-7862 (fax)
http://www.cbs.state.or.us/external/dfcs
- Richard M. ("Dick") Nockelby
  Administrator
  richard.m.nockleby@state.or.us
- James G. Harlan
  Deputy Administrator
  503/947-7478
  james.g.harlan@state.or.us

PENNSYLVANIA

Securities Commission
Eastgate Office Building
1010 North 7th Street, 2nd Floor
Harrisburg, Pennsylvania 17102-1410
717/787-8061
717/783-5122 (fax)
http://www.psc.state.pa.us
• Robert M. Lam
  Chairman
  717/787-6828

Philadelphia office:
State Office Building
Suite 1100
Philadelphia, Pennsylvania 19130-4088
215/560-2088
215/560-3977 (fax)

Pittsburgh office:
806 State Office Building
Pittsburgh, Pennsylvania 15222-1210
412/565-5083
412/565-7647 (fax)

RHODE ISLAND

Department of Business Regulation
Securities Division
233 Richmond Street, Suite 232
Providence, Rhode Island 02903-4232
401/222-3048
401/222-5629 (fax)
secdiv@dbr.state.ri.us
http://www.doa.state.ri.us
• Maria D'Alessandro Piccirilli
   Associate Director and Superintendent of Securities
   mpicciri@dbr.state.ri.us

SOUTH CAROLINA

Office of the Attorney General
Securities Division
Rembert C. Dennis Office Building
1000 Assembly Street
Columbia, South Carolina 29201
Mailing address: P.O. Box 11549
Columbia, South Carolina 29211-1549
803/734-4731
803/734-0032 (fax)
agsecurities@ag.state.sc.us (e-mail)
http://www.scattorneygeneral.org
• David Jonson
   Deputy Attorney General/Deputy Securities
   803/734-4731
   agdjonson@ag.state.sc.us

SOUTH DAKOTA

Division of Securities
118 West Capitol Avenue
Pierre, South Dakota 57501-2000
605/773-4823
605/773-5953 (fax)
securities@crpr1.state.sd.us (e-mail)
http://www.state.sd.us/dcr/securities
* Gail Sheppick
   Director
   Gail.Sheppick@state.sd.us

TENNESSEE

Department of Commerce and Insurance
Securities Division
Davy Crockett Tower, Suite 680
500 James Robertson Parkway
Nashville, Tennessee 37243-0575
615/741-2947
615/532-8375 (fax)
http://www.state.tn.us/commerce/securdiv.html
* Daphne D. Smith
   Assistant Commissioner for Securities
   dsmith3@mail.state.tn.us

TEXAS

State Securities Board
208 East 10th Street, 5th Floor
Austin, Texas 78701
Mailing address: P.O. Box 13167
Austin, Texas 78711-3167
512/305-8300
512/305-8310 (fax)
http://www.ssb.state.tx.us
• Denise Voigt Crawford
  Securities Commissioner
  512/305-8306
  512/305-8336 (fax)
  dcrawford@ssb.state.tx.us

UTAH

Division of Securities
Heber M. Wells Building
160 East 300 South, 2nd Floor
Salt Lake City, Utah 84111
Mailing address: P.O. Box 146760
Salt Lake City, Utah 84114-6760
801/530-6600
801/530-6980 (fax)
security@br.state.ut.us (e-mail)
http://www.commerce.state.ut.us
• S. Anthony ("Tony") Taggart
  Director, Securities Division

VERMONT

Department of Banking, Insurance, Securities, and Health Care Administration
Securities Division
89 Main Street, 2nd Floor
Montpelier, Vermont 05620
Mailing address: 89 Main Street
Drawer 20
Montpelier, Vermont 05620-3101
802/828-3420
802/828-2896 (fax)
http://www.state.vt.us/bis
• Blythe McLaughlin
  Deputy Commissioner
  bmclaughlin@bishca.state.vt.us

VIRGINIA

State Corporation Commission
Division of Securities and Retail Franchising
1300 East Main Street, 9th Floor
Richmond, Virginia 23219
Mailing address: P.O. Box 1197
Richmond, Virginia 23218
804/371-9051
804/371-9911 (fax)
http://www.state.va.us/scc/division/srf
• Ronald W. Thomas
  Director
  804/371-9006
  rthomas@scc.state.va.us

WASHINGTON

Department of Financial Institutions
Securities Division
General Administration Building
210 11th Street
3rd Floor West, Room 300
Olympia, Washington 98504-1200
Mailing address: P.O. Box 9033
Olympia, Washington 98507-9033
360/902-8760
360/586-5068 (fax)
http://www.wa.gov/dfi/securities
• Deborah R. Bortner
  Director of Securities
  360/902-8797
  360/704-6997 (fax)
  dbortner@dfi.wa.gov

WEST VIRGINIA

Office of the State Auditor
Securities Division
Building 1, Room W-100
Charleston, West Virginia 25305
304/558-2257
304/558-4211 (fax)
http://www.wvauditor.com
securities@wvauditor.com (e-mail)
• Chester F. Thompson
  Deputy Commissioner of Securities

WISCONSIN

Department of Financial Institutions
Division of Securities
345 W. Washington Avenue, 4th Floor
Madison, Wisconsin 53703
Mailing address: P.O. Box 1768
Madison, Wisconsin 53701-1768
608/261-9555
608/256-1259 (fax)
http://badger.state.wi.us/agencies/dfi
- Patricia D. Struck
  Administrator
  608/266-3432
  patricia.struck@dfi.state.wi.us

WYOMING

Secretary of State
Securities Division
State Capitol, Room 109
200 West 24th Street
Cheyenne, Wyoming 82002-0020
307/777-7370
307/777-5339 (fax)
securities@state.wy.us (e-mail)
http://www.soswy.state.wy.us
- Thomas Cowan
  Division Director
  tcowan@state.wy.us

PUERTO RICO

Commissioner of Financial Institutions
P.O. Box 11855
Fernandez Juncos Station
San Juan, Puerto Rico 00910-3855
787/723-3131
787/723-4225 (fax)
• Felipe B. Cruz
  Assistant Commissioner
  Extension 2222 or 2214

CANADA

ALBERTA

Securities Commission
300 5th Avenue S.W., 4th Floor
Calgary, Alberta
Canada T2P 3C4
403/297-6454
403/297-6156 (fax)
http://www.albertasecurities.com
• Stephen P. Sibold, Q.C.
  Chair
  403/297-4280
  403/297-4486 (fax)
  stephen.sibold@seccom.ab.ca

BRITISH COLUMBIA

Securities Commission
200-865 Hornby Street
Vancouver, British Columbia
Canada V6Z 2H4
604/899-6500
604/899-6506 (fax)
604/899-6550 (Insider Reporting fax)
http://www.bcsc.bc.ca
* Adrienne Wanstall
  Commissioner
  604/899-6536
  awanstall@bcsc.bc.ca

MANITOBA

Securities Commission
1130-405 Broadway
Winnipeg, Manitoba
Canada R3C 3L6
204/945-2548
204/945-0330 (fax)
* Donald G. Murray
  Chairman
  204/945-2551
  dmurray@cca.gov.mb.ca

NEW BRUNSWICK

Securities Administration Branch
133 Prince William Street, Suite 606
Harbour Building
Saint John, New Brunswick
Canada E2L 4Y9
Mailing address: P.O. Box 5001
133 Prince William Street
Suite 606
Saint John, New Brunswick
Canada E2L 4Y9
506/658-3060
506/658-3059 (fax)
• Donne W. Smith, Jr.
  Administrator
  donne.smith@gov.nb.ca

NEWFOUNDLAND AND LABRADOR

Department of Government Services and Lands
Securities Division
Confederation Building
West Block, 2nd Floor
St. John's, Newfoundland
Mailing address: P.O. Box 8700
St. John's, Newfoundland
Canada A1B 4J6
709/729-4189
709/729-6187 (fax)
• Anthony W. Patey
  Director of Securities
  709/729-4189

NORTHWEST TERRITORIES

Securities Registry
Department of Justice
Stuart M. Hodgson Building
5009 49th Street, 1st Floor
Yellowknife, Northwest Territories
Canada X1A 2L9
867/873-7490
867/873-0243 (fax)
• Katharine Tummon
  Registrar of Securities

NOVA SCOTIA

Securities Commission
Joseph Howe Building
1690 Hollis Street, 2nd Floor
Halifax, Nova Scotia
Canada B3J 3J9
Mailing address: P.O. Box 458
Halifax, Nova Scotia
Canada B3H 2P8
902/424-7768
902/424-4625 (fax)
hiscocbr@gov.ns.ca (e-mail)
• Robert B. MacLellan
  Chairman

NUNAVUT

Legal Registries
Bag 9500
5102 50th Avenue, Suite 2
Lower Level, Scotia Center
Yellowknife, NT
Canada X1A 2R3
867/920-6354
867/873-0586 (fax)
http://www.gov.nt.ca
• Gary Crowe
  Acting Director
  gary_crowe@gov.nt.ca

ONTARIO

Securities Commission
20 Queen Street West, Suite 800
Box 55
Toronto, Ontario
Canada M5H 3S8
416/597-0681
416/593-8241 (fax)
• Howard I. Wetston, Q.C.
  Vice-Chair Securities Commission Administrator
  416/593-8206
  416/593-8241 (fax)
  hwetston@osc.gov.on.ca

PRINCE EDWARD ISLAND

Department of Community Services and Attorney General
95 Rochford Street, 4th Floor
Charlottetown, Prince Edward Island
Canada C1A 7N8
902/368-4552
902/368-5283 (fax)
http://www.gov.pe.ca
- Edison Shea
  Registrar of Securities
  ejshea@gov.pe.ca

QUÉBEC

Commission des valeurs mobilières du Québec
800 Square Victoria, 22nd Floor
P.O. Box 246
Tour de la Bourse
Stock Exchange Tower
Montreal, Québec
Canada H4Z 1G3
514/940-2150
514/873-3090 (fax: Staff/Operations)
514/873-4130 (fax: Enforcement)
514/873-0711 (fax: Commissioner's Office)
courrier@cvmq.gouv.qc.ca (e-mail)
http://www.cvmq.com
- Marie Noelle Berube
  Chief, International Affairs
  marie-noelle.berube@cvmq.com

SASKATCHEWAN

Securities Commission
800 1920 Broad Street
Regina, Saskatchewan
Canada S4P 3V7
306/787-5645
306/787-5899 (fax)
ssc@govmail.gov.sk.ca (e-mail)
* Marcel de la Gorgendiere, Q.C.
  Chairman
  306/787-5630
  mdelagorgendiere@ssc.gov.sk.ca

YUKON TERRITORY

Corporate Affairs
2134 2nd Avenue, 3rd Floor
Andrew A. Philipsen Law Centre
Whitehorse, Yukon
Canada Y1A 5H3
Mailing address: Corporate Affairs J-9
P.O. Box 2703
Whitehorse, Yukon
Canada Y1A 2C6
867/667-5225
867/393-6251 (fax)
* M. Richard Roberts
  Registrar of Securities
  richard.roberts@gov.yk.ca

MEXICO

COMISIÓN NACIONAL BANCARIA Y DE VALORES

International Affairs General Direction
Insurgentes Sur 1971
Torre Sur, Piso 9, Plaza Inn
Col. Guadalupe Inn
Mexico, D.F. 01020
011 525/724-6578, 6571
011 525/724-6220 (fax)
* Miguel Angel Garza
Director General (International Affairs)

Appendix

B

SEC FILINGS

This appendix offers a fairly extensive list of SEC forms and their descriptions. Most of these forms are filed electronically on EDGAR. For a complete list, go to the SEC's forms page within its site: http://www.sec.gov/edaux/forms.htm.

These descriptions may, from time to time, be overruled by the SEC's interpretation of the rules and regulations governing securities. This appendix cannot be used as a "legal reference document."

Annual Report to Shareholders

The Annual Report to Shareholders is the principal document used by most public companies to disclose corporate information to shareholders. It is usually a state-of-the-company report that includes an opening letter from the Chief Executive Officer, financial data, results of continuing operations, market segment information, new product plans, subsidiary activities, and research and development activities directed toward future programs.

Source: Securities and Exchange Commission.

Securities Act Forms

Form BD

This form is used to apply for registration as a broker or dealer of securities or as a government securities broker or dealer, and to amend a registration. It provides background information on the applicant and the nature of its business. The names of the executive officers and general partners of the company are listed. Information on any past securities violations is provided.

Form D

Companies selling securities in reliance on a Regulation D exemption or a Section 4(6) exemption from the registration provisions of the Securities Act of 1933 ("the 1933 Act") must file Form D as notice of such a sale. The form must be filed no later than 15 days after the first sale of securities.

Form 1-A

Regulation A provides the basis for an exemption for certain small offerings (generally, up to $5 million in any twelve-month period). Companies selling securities in reliance on a Regulation A exemption from the registration provisions of the 1933 Act must provide investors with an offering statement that meets the requirements of Form 1-A.

Prospectus

The prospectus constitutes Part I of the 1933 Act registration statement. It contains the basic business and financial information on an issuer, with respect to a particular securities offering. Investors may use the prospectus to help them appraise the merits of the offering and make educated investment decisions.

A prospectus in its preliminary form is frequently called a *"red herring" prospectus* and is subject to completion or amendment before the registration statement becomes effective. A final prospectus is then issued, and sales can be consummated.

Proxy Solicitation Materials
(Regulation 14A/Schedule 14A)

State law governs the circumstances under which shareholders are entitled to vote. When a shareholder vote is required and any person solicits proxies with respect to securities registered under Section 12 of the Securities and Exchange Act of 1934 ("the 1934 Act"), that person generally is required to furnish a proxy statement containing the information specified by Schedule 14A. The proxy statement is intended to provide security holders with the information necessary to enable them to vote in an informed manner on matters intended to be acted upon at security holders' meetings, whether the traditional annual meeting or a special meeting. Typically, a security holder is also provided with a "proxy card" to authorize designated persons to vote his or her securities on the security holder's behalf, in the event the holder does not vote in person at the meeting. Copies of definitive (final) proxy statements and proxy cards are filed with the SEC at the time they are sent to security holders. For further information about the applicability of the SEC's proxy rules, see Section 14(a) of the 1934 Act and Regulation 14A.

Certain preliminary proxy filings relating to mergers, consolidations, acquisitions, and similar matters are nonpublic upon filing; all other proxy filings are publicly available.

1933 Act Registration Statements

One of the major purposes of the federal securities laws is to require companies making a public offering of securities to disclose material business and financial information in order that investors may make informed investment decisions. The 1933 Act requires issuers to file registration statements with the SEC, setting forth such information, before offering their securities to the public. (See Section 6 of the 1933 Act for information concerning the "Registration of Securities and Signing of Registration Statement." Section 8 of the 1933 Act gives information on "Taking Effect of Registration Statements and Amendments Thereto.")

The registration statement is divided into two parts. Part I, the prospectus, is distributed to interested investors and others. It contains data to assist in evaluating the securities and to make informed investment decisions.

Part II of the registration statement contains information not required to be in the prospectus, for example: the registrants' expenses of issuance and distribution, indemnification of directors and officers, and recent sales of unregistered securities as well as undertakings and copies of material contracts.

(Investment companies file 1933 Act registration statements that are, in many cases, also registration statements under the Investment Company Act of 1940. Descriptions of registration statements filed by these issuers are given in the following section.)

Interpretive Responsibility

Division of Corporation Finance, Office of Chief Counsel. [For the foreign forms (e.g., F-1, F-2, etc.), the Office of International Corporate Finance should be consulted.]

The most widely used 1933 Act registration forms are as follows:

S-1	This is the basic registration form. It can be used to register securities for which no other form is authorized or prescribed, except securities of foreign governments or political subdivisions thereof.
S-2	This is a simplified optional registration form that may be used by companies that have been required to report under the 1934 Act for a minimum of three years and have timely filed all required reports during the twelve calendar months and any portion of the month immediately preceding the filing of the registration statement. Unlike Form S-1, Form S-2 permits incorporation by reference from the company's annual report to stockholders (or annual report on Form 10-K) and periodic reports. Delivery of these incorporated documents (as well as the prospectus) to investors may be required.
S-3	This is the most simplified registration form. It may be used only by companies that have been

	required to report under the 1934 Act for a minimum of twelve months and have met the timely filing requirements set forth under Form S-2. Also, the offering and issuer must meet the eligibility tests prescribed by the form. The form maximizes incorporating by reference information from the 1934 Act filings.
S-4	This form is used to register securities in connection with business combinations and exchange offers.
S-8	This form is used for the registration of securities to be offered to an issuer's employees pursuant to certain plans.
S-11	This form is used to register securities of certain real estate companies, including real estate investment trusts.
SB-1	This form may be used by certain "small business issuers" to register offerings of up to $10 million of securities, provided that the company has not registered more than $10 million in securities offerings during the preceding twelve months. This form requires less detailed information about the issuer's business than Form S-1. Generally, a "small business issuer" is a U.S. or Canadian company with revenues and public market float less than $25 million.
SB-2	This form may be used by "small business issuers" to register securities to be sold for cash. The form requires less detailed information about the issuer's business than Form S-1.

(continued)

(Continued)

S-20	This form may be used to register standardized options where the issuer undertakes not to issue, clear, guarantee, or accept an option registered on Form S-20 unless there is a definitive options disclosure document meeting the requirements of Rule 9b-1 of the 1934 Act.
Sch B	Schedule B is the registration statement used by foreign governments (or political subdivisions of foreign governments) to register securities. Generally, it contains a description of the country and its government, the terms of the offering, and the uses of proceeds.
F-1	This is the basic registration form authorized for certain foreign private issuers. It is used to register the securities of those eligible foreign issuers for which no other more specialized form is authorized or prescribed.
F-2	This is an optional registration form that may be used by certain foreign private issuers that have an equity float of at least $75 million worldwide or are registering nonconvertible investment grade securities or have reported under the 1934 Act for a minimum of three years. The form is somewhat shorter than Form F-1 because it uses delivery of filings made by the issuer under the 1934 Act, particularly Form 20-F.
F-3	This form may be used only by certain foreign private issuers that have reported under the 1934 Act for a minimum of twelve months and have a worldwide public market float of more than $75 million.

	The form also may be used by eligible foreign private issuers to register offerings of nonconvertible investment-grade securities, securities to be sold by selling security holders, or securities to be issued to certain existing security holders. The form allows the 1934 Act filings to be incorporated by reference.
F-4	This form is used to register securities in connection with business combinations and exchange offers involving foreign private issuers.
F-6	This form is used to register depository shares represented by American Depository Receipts ("ADRs") issued by a depository against the deposit of the securities of a foreign issuer.
F-7	This form is used by certain eligible publicly traded Canadian foreign private issuers to register rights offers extended to their U.S. shareholders. The form acts as a wraparound for the relevant Canadian offering documents. To be registered on Form F-7, the rights must be granted to U.S. shareholders on terms no less favorable than those extended to other shareholders.
F-8	This form may be used by eligible, large, publicly traded Canadian foreign private issuers to register securities offered in business combinations and exchange offers. The form acts as a wraparound for the relevant Canadian offering or disclosure documents. The securities must be offered to U.S. holders on terms no less favorable than those extended to other holders.

(continued)

(Continued)

F-9	This form may be used by eligible, large, publicly traded Canadian foreign private issuers to register nonconvertible investment-grade securities. Form F-9 acts as a wraparound for the relevant Canadian offering documents.
F-10	This form may be used by eligible, large, publicly traded Canadian foreign private issuers to register any securities (except certain derivative securities). The form acts as a wraparound for the relevant Canadian offering documents. Unlike Forms F-7, F-8, F-9, and F-80, however, Form F-10 requires the Canadian issuer to reconcile its financial statements to the U.S. Generally Accepted Accounting Principles (GAAP).
F-80	This form may be used by eligible, large, publicly traded Canadian foreign private issuers to register securities offered in business combinations and exchange offers. The form acts as a wraparound for the relevant Canadian offering or disclosure documents. The securities must be offered to U.S. holders on terms no less favorable than those extended to other holders.
SR	This form is used, by first-time registrants under the Act, as a report of sales of registered securities and use of proceeds therefrom. The form is required at specified periods of time throughout the offering period, and a final report is required after the termination of the offering.
S-6	This form is used to register securities issued by unit investment trusts (the 1933 Act only).

Other Securities Act Forms

Form 144

This form must be filed as a notice of the proposed sale of restricted securities or securities held by an affiliate of the issuer in reliance on Rule 144, when the amount to be sold during any three-month period exceeds 500 shares or units or has an aggregate sales price in excess of $10,000.

Interpretive Responsibility

Division of Corporation Finance, Office of Chief Counsel.

1934 Act Registration Statements

All companies with securities registered on a national securities exchange, and, in general, other companies with total assets exceeding $10 million and with a class of equity securities held by 500 or more persons, must register such securities under the 1934 Act. (See Section 12 of the 1934 Act for further information.)

This registration establishes a public file containing material financial and business information on the company for use by investors and others. It also creates an obligation on the part of the company to keep such public information current by filing periodic reports on Forms 10-Q and 10-K, and on current event Form 8-K, as applicable.

In addition, if registration under the 1934 Act is not required, any issuer who conducts a public offering of securities must file reports for the year in which it conducts the offering (and in subsequent years, if the securities are held by more than 300 holders).

The most widely used 1934 Act registration forms are as follows:

10	This is the general form for registration of securities pursuant to Section 12(b) or 12(g) of the 1934 Act of classes of securities of issuers for which no other form is prescribed. It requires certain business and financial information about the issuer.
10-SB	This is the general form for registration of securities pursuant to Section 12(b) or 12(g) of the 1934 Act for "small business issuers." This form requires slightly less detailed information about the company's business than Form 10.
8-A	This optional short form may be used by companies to register securities under the 1934 Act.
8-B	This specialized registration form may be used by certain issuers with no securities registered under the 1934 Act that succeed to another issuer which had securities so registered at the time of succession.
20-F	This is an integrated form used both as a registration statement for purposes of registering securities of qualified foreign private issuers under Section 12 and as an annual report under Section 13(a) or 15(d) of the 1934 Act.
40-F	This is an integrated form used both as a registration statement to register securities of eligible publicly traded Canadian foreign private issuers or as an annual report for such issuers. It serves as a wraparound for the company's Canadian public reports.

Other Exchange Act Forms

Form TA-1

This form is used to apply for registration as a transfer agent or to amend such registration. It provides information on the company's activities and operation.

Interpretive Responsibility

Division of Market Regulation, Branch of Stock Surveillance.

Form X-17A-5

Every broker or dealer registered pursuant to Section 15 of the Exchange Act must file annually, on a calendar or fiscal year basis, a report audited by an independent public accountant.

Interpretive Responsibility

Division of Market Regulation, Branch of Financial Reporting.

Forms 3, 4, and 5

Every director, officer, or owner of more than ten percent of a class of equity securities registered under Section 12 of the 1934 Act must file with the SEC a statement of ownership regarding such securities. The initial filing is on Form 3, and changes are reported on Form 4. The Annual Statement of beneficial ownership of securities is on Form 5. The forms require information on the reporting person's relationship to the company and on purchases and sales of such equity securities.

Interpretive Responsibility

Division of Corporation Finance, Office of Chief Counsel.

Form 8-K

This is the "current report" that is used to report the occurrence of any material events or corporate changes that are of importance to investors or security holders and previously have not been reported by the registrant. It provides more current information on certain specified events than would Forms 10-Q or 10-K.

Form 10-C

This form must be filed by an issuer whose securities are quoted on the Nasdaq interdealer quotation system. Reported on the form is any change, in excess of 5 percent, in the number of shares of the class outstanding, and any change in the name of the issuer. The report must be filed within ten days of such change.

Form 10-K

This is the annual report that most reporting companies file with the SEC. It provides a comprehensive overview of the registrant's business. The report must be filed within 90 days after the end of the company's fiscal year.

Form 10-KSB

This is the annual report filed by reporting "small business issuers." It provides a comprehensive overview of the company's business, although its requirements call for slightly less detailed information than is required by Form 10-K. The report must be filed within 90 days after the end of the company's fiscal year.

Form 10-Q

This report is filed quarterly by most reporting companies. It includes unaudited financial statements and provides a continuing view of the company's financial position during the year. The report must be filed for each of the first three fiscal quarters of the company's fiscal year and is due within 45 days of the close of the quarter.

Form 10-QSB

This form must be filed quarterly by reporting small business issuers. It includes unaudited financial statements and provides a continuing view of the company's financial position and the results of its operations throughout the year. The report must be filed for each of the first three fiscal quarters and is due within 45 days of the close of each quarter.

Form 11-K

This form is a special annual report for employee stock purchase, savings, and similar plans, interests in which constitute securities registered under the 1933 Act. The report is required in addition to any other annual report of the issuer of the securities (e.g., a company's annual report to all shareholders, or Form 10-K).

Form 15

This form is filed by a company as a notice of termination of registration under Section 12(g) of the 1934 Act, or suspension of the duty to file periodic reports under Sections 13 and 15(d) of the 1934 Act.

Schedule 13D

This schedule discloses beneficial ownership of certain registered equity securities. Any person (or group of persons) who acquires a beneficial ownership of more than 5 percent of a class of registered equity securities of certain issuers must file a Schedule 13D, reporting such acquisition together with certain other information, within ten days after such acquisition. Moreover, any material changes in the facts set forth in the schedule generally precipitate a duty to promptly file an amendment on Schedule 13D. The SEC rules define the term "beneficial owner" to be any person who directly or indirectly shares voting power or investment power (the power to sell the security).

Schedule 13E-4

This schedule (called an Issuer Tender Offer Statement) must be filed by certain reporting companies that make tender offers for their own securities. Rule 13E-4 under the 1934 Act imposes additional requirements than an issuer must comply with when making an issuer tender offer.

Information Statement
(Regulation 14C/Schedule 14C)

Schedule 14C sets forth the disclosure requirements for information statements. Generally, a company with securities registered under Section 12 of the 1934 Act must send an information statement to every holder of the registered security who is entitled to vote on any matter for which the company is not soliciting proxies. (If the company solicits proxies, Regulation 14C/Schedule 14A may be required.)

Appendix

C

SEC Regional Offices

SEC Headquarters
Securities and Exchange Commission
450 Fifth Street, NW
Washington, DC 20549
Office of Investor Education and Assistance
202/942-7040
E-mail: help@sec.gov

Northeast Regional Office
Securities and Exchange Commission
Carmen J. Lawrence, Regional Director
7 World Trade Center, Suite 1300
New York, NY 10048
212/748-8000
E-mail: newyork@sec.gov

Boston District Office
Securities and Exchange Commission
Juan M. Marcelino, District Administrator
73 Tremont Street, Suite 600
Boston, MA 02108-3912
617/424-5900
E-mail: boston@sec.gov

Source: Securities and Exchange Commission.

Philadelphia District Office

Securities and Exchange Commission
Ronald C. Long, District Administrator
The Curtis Center, Suite 1120E
601 Walnut Street
Philadelphia, PA 19106-3322
215/597-3100
E-mail: philadelphia@sec.gov

Southeast Regional Office

Securities and Exchange Commission
Randall J. Fons, Regional Director
1401 Brickell Avenue, Suite 200
Miami, FL 33131
305/536-4700
E-mail: miami@sec.gov

Atlanta District Office

Securities and Exchange Commission
Richard P. Wessel, District Administrator
3475 Lenox Road, NE, Suite 1000
Atlanta, GA 30326-1232
404/842-7600
E-mail: atlanta@sec.gov

Midwest Regional Office

Securities and Exchange Commission
Mary Keefe, Regional Director
Citicorp Center, Suite 1400
500 W. Madison Street
Chicago, IL 60661-2511
312/353-7390
E-mail: chicago@sec.gov

Central Regional Office
Securities and Exchange Commission
Daniel F. Shea, Regional Director
1801 California Street, Suite 4800
Denver, CO 80202-2648
303/844-1000
E-mail: denver@sec.gov

Fort Worth District Office
Securities and Exchange Commission
Harold F. Degenhardt, District Administrator
801 Cherry Street, 19th Floor
Fort Worth, TX 76102
817/978-3821
E-mail: dfw@sec.gov

Salt Lake District Office
Securities and Exchange Commission
Kenneth D. Israel, Jr., District Administrator
50 South Main Street, Suite 500
Salt Lake City, UT 84144-0402
801/524-5796
E-mail: saltlake@sec.gov

Pacific Regional Office
Securities and Exchange Commission
Valerie Caproni, Regional Director
5670 Wilshire Boulevard, 11th Floor
Los Angeles, CA 90036-3648
323/965-3998
E-mail: losangeles@sec.gov

San Francisco District Office
Securities and Exchange Commission
Helane Morrison, District Administrator
44 Montgomery Street, Suite 1100
San Francisco, CA 94104
415/705-2500
E-mail: sanfrancisco@sec.gov

Appendix

D

NASDAQ LISTING REQUIREMENTS

Nasdaq's listing requirements are extensive and detailed. The following includes the main quantitative measures that a company must meet in order to qualify for Nasdaq National Market trading. For a complete guide to the National Market listing requirements and for details of the Nasdaq's Small Cap listing requirements, go to Nasdaq's listing page, http://www.nasdaq.com/about/listing.stm.

4420. Quantitative Designation Criteria

In order to be designated for the Nasdaq National Market, an issuer shall be required to substantially meet the criteria set forth in paragraphs (a), (b), (c), (d), (e), (f), or (g) below. Initial Public Offerings substantially meeting such criteria are eligible for immediate inclusion in the Nasdaq National Market upon prior application and with the written consent of the managing underwriter that immediate inclusion is desired. All other qualifying issues, excepting special situations, are included on the next inclusion date established by Nasdaq.

Source: National Association of Securities Dealers.

(a) Entry Standard 1

   (1) The issuer of the security had annual pre-tax income of at least $1,000,000 in the most recently completed fiscal year or in two of the last three most recently completed fiscal years.

   (2) There are at least 1,100,000 publicly held shares.

   (3) The market value of publicly held shares is at least $8 million.

   (4) The bid price per share is $5 or more.

   (5) The issuer of the security has net tangible assets of at least $6 million.

   (6) The issuer has a minimum of 400 round lot shareholders.

   (7) There are at least three registered and active Market Makers with respect to the security.

(b) Entry Standard 2

   (1) The issuer of the security has net tangible assets of at least $18 million.

   (2) There are at least 1,100,000 publicly held shares.

   (3) The market value of publicly held shares is at least $18 million.

   (4) The bid price per share is $5 or more.

   (5) There are at least three registered and active Market Makers with respect to the security.

   (6) The issuer has a two-year operating history.

   (7) The issuer has a minimum of 400 round lot shareholders.

Appendix

E

WEB SITE REVIEWS

Stock Detective's Guide to Safe and Profitable Surfing

The amount of financial information on the Internet can be awfully intimidating for investors. This appendix will help you find what you need without overlooking a lot of the really useful resources or falling prey to unscrupulous promoters or misinformed amateurs.

If you read any of the leading financial magazines, chances are you've already read somebody else's list of recommended Web sites. Nevertheless, in appreciation of your kindness in buying our book, we felt obligated to provide you with our own list—the way Stock Detective views things, that is. Following are sites we've visited or use ourselves. We surely have overlooked a few more that are worthwhile and scrupulous, but there's only so much time—yours and ours.

Barron's Online (www.barrons.com).   Here's a hint: If you subscribe to *Barron's* in the print edition and you can do without much of the week-old market laboratory, then save some money and cancel your subscription. You can get all the rest of *Barron's* online for free, including Alan Abelson's quintessential "Up and Down Wall Street" column, and more.

Bloomberg (www.bloomberg.com).   Most investors are familiar with at least one part of the Bloomberg financial information empire. Bloomberg television, Bloomberg radio, Bloomberg "the magazine," Bloomberg news wires, the

Bloomberg Web site, and of course what Bloomberg often refers to as "The Bloomberg," a dedicated online service for which professional traders and money managers often pay over $25,000 per year to receive. As for the Bloomberg Web site: Ho-hum; nothing really special here. Did you think Bloomberg was gonna give away the store for free? All those great, original Bloomberg news stories—not here, folks. One tip: If you follow a particular stock, you may want to check its quote/news page here. Bloomberg news articles do become available on related stocks, but only for a day or two. Then they get archived to the pay-for-Bloomberg service.

Briefing.com (www.briefing.com). Briefing.com offers a useful mix of free and subscription-based features. Included in the free features are daily upgrades and downgrades, stock splits and economic calendars, plus up-to-the-minute market news and analysts' commentary. For $9.95 up to $25 per month, you can get live analysis, live upgrades and downgrades, earnings calendars, and individual stock analyses.

CBS MarketWatch (cbs.marketwatch.com). With its purchase of the charting site called Big Charts, its origins with quote server Data Broadcasting, and its news culture and brand alliance with CBS, this is one of the most extensive and useful Web sites for investors today. If there's any criticism, it has to be that there's too much news and commentary. Many regular columns are hard to find if they somehow don't merit placement on the vaunted home page. Quotes and charts are excellent too. One unique feature is after-hours trading quotes. Many widely followed stocks trade in after-hours markets and indicate to investors what might be expected at the next day's opening. Another great feature: the options quotes on stocks. We've found that few sites offer reliable and easy-to-use option quotes for free. This is one of them.

CNNfn (www.cnnfn.com). News network CNN's finance site is pretty much what you'd expect: a news site. A very good financial news site. CNNfn is especially useful for when you need up-to-the-minute news or fast-breaking stories.

Free EDGAR (www.freeedgar.com). This is the best free Web site for finding and reading SEC filings. Loading is a little slow, and sometimes it's hard to locate certain filings, but this site has no competition without paying a fee. Free EDGAR is comprehensive and well organized. One of the best features is that it lets users determine the font (text) size when they wish to view filing documents. This is especially useful because many filings are quite lengthy and contain wide tables. Another neat feature is an option to download the files in RTF (rich text format), which allows most users to save a document as a word processing file on their own computers. We've found one strange quirk that is annoying. If you're looking for filings for OTCBB-listed stocks, you'll need to search by company name rather than by symbol. If the company is a dot-com, just spell out the part of the name before "dot." Ironically, Edgar Online, the only other pay site that competes with Free EDGAR, has bought Free EDGAR.

Free Real Time (www.freerealtime.com). Unlimited free real time stock quotes, watch lists, news, charts, and more. If you like your stock quotes in real time and don't feel like using up your real time quote allotment at your brokerage site, this is the place for you. You have to register (free) to get real time stock quotes, and the demand for real time quotes can get intense at times, especially near open and close and during volatile market sessions, so there may be user log jams and outages. If you depend on reliable real time quotes, it's a good idea to register at one or two other real time quote sites as a backup. Thomson Investor (www.thomsoninvest.net) and FinancialWeb (www.financialweb.com) both offer free real time quote servers.

Gomez.com (www.gomez.com). Gomez.com is not a financial information site. You won't get stock quotes, charts, and news here. It's a Web site that provides research for online consumers. What online investors do get from Gomez is, perhaps, the best research on and comparison of online brokers anywhere. Gomez even compares and scores brokers differently, based on what kind of customer you are—for example, hyperactive traders to conservative retirement planners. Before you pick, or change, your online broker, you must visit Gomez.com.

Hoover's (www.hoovers.com). Hoover's is one of the oldest and most comprehensive Web sites for fundamental company research. Hoover's provides capsules as well as detailed financial and corporate information on thousands of public and private corporations. Hoover's also provides comprehensive IPO information, and other features and tools that make it a top-notch research and news site for investors. Beware, however, that all is not free on Hoover's. If you want unlimited access to all Hoover's hand-crafted research, you'll need to pay $14.95 a month, but there's still enough free stuff to satisfy most investors' needs.

Individual Investor Online (www.iionline.com). Brought to you by the same people who publish *Individual Investor* magazine, this Web site provides a wealth of stock picks and stock ideas. You can follow the daily progress of the magazine's annual "Magic 25" stock-pick list or check out the "Stock of the Day."

Investor Words (www.investorwords.com). This is an interesting site worthy of any investor's financial bookmarks. Investor Words is one huge glossary for—you guessed it—investment terms. The site boasts over 5,000 investment-related definitions and over 15,000 links between related terms. With that many definitions, the site is sometimes overwhelming, but if you know what word or term you're seeking, it's a breeze. The related-term linking is extremely useful for expanding your lexicon of investment words.

Investorama (www.investorama.com). Author Douglas Gerlach has been compiling links to useful Web sites longer then most of us have owned Internet-ready computers. Investorama is built around a search engine for stocks. Enter a stock symbol and you'll get a page containing hundreds of links to pages on dozens of leading sites relating exactly to that particular stock. But hang around the site a little longer for the articles, reviews, guides, and directories to hundreds of related financial sites. Be careful, however. Investorama does not filter out penny-stock promoter sites from its guides and directories. That's your job.

IPO.com (www.ipo.com). If you're interested in initial public offerings, IPO.com is, far and away, the best and most useful Web site. It features a wealth of up-to-date information about recent and upcoming IPOs in easy-to-use, detailed form. In addition, the site offers concise and useful IPO news, commentary, and analysis.

Market Guide (www.marketguide.com). Market Guide is best known for its free and comprehensive company profiles.

Each profile is quite detailed and up-to-date, and includes information on company earnings, institutional ownership, insider trading, and much more. Another useful feature of the site is the downloadable spreadsheets that contain lists of stocks based on prescreened criteria.

Money.com (www.money.com). The official site of *Money* magazine, Money.com is a close sister to its off-line namesake. As you'd expect, there are lots and lots of articles, "how to's," and "best of's," just like the magazine, plus a lot of non-stock-market content targeted to well-heeled consumers focusing on automobiles, insurance, real estate, and retirement. A nice site with plenty to read and do—thankfully, for free.

MSN Money Central (www.money.com). Another great super site. Money Central is one of the most comprehensive financial sites around. Money Central features original news and analysis; excellent quoting, charting, and stock screening tools; and a lot more. One little bummer, however: You have to download some Microsoft software in order to use the charts or screening tools.

Multex Investor (www.multex.com). Multex is really two sites: (1) a free site, called Multex Investor and (2) the original pay service known as Multex. Multex is in the business of aggregating brokerage analysts' reports. Most of these reports are reserved only for the clients of those brokerages, so you won't be able to find them very easily anywhere else. If you want unlimited access to as many of these reports as possible, the Multex pay service may be for you. The Multex Investor site offers research reports for free, but those tend to be limited to a smaller number of large brokerage firms that have paid Multex to help promote their services. Unfortunately, if you want to get a free report, you'll probably have to submit a registration form to each and every firm offering a report, and then you'll have to put up with their e-mail solicitations.

North American Securities Administrators Association (www.nasaa.org). This is the site of the nonprofit organization that represents state and federal regulators throughout the United States and Canada. You'll find useful investor education materials and timely news articles here. Many warn about investment fraud.

On Money (www.onmoney.com). Not content with being just another financial news, quotes, and ideas site, On Money adds a special gimmick. The site allows you to consolidate many of your existing online accounts into one portfolio, provided that your bank, credit card company, online broker, and so on, participate with On Money.

Raging Bull (www.ragingbull.com). If you're into stock message boards, this is the site for you. Raging Bull not only boasts the largest community of stock message board participants, but it also has some of the most useful features, including an "ignore" feature that let's you tune out members you'd prefer not to deal with. Adding to its popularity, Raging Bull is completely free. A word of extreme caution to anyone who uses these message boards: Don't accept anything you read as truthful. Raging Bull's message boards, like other message boards, are entertaining and useful, but sometimes can contain relentless hype, fraud, or just plain fiction. You should still do some of your own homework before making an investment decision; don't use the message board as your sole resource.

Silicon Investor (www.techstocks.com). Once the crown prince of message board sites, SI (as it's affectionately known to regulars) has become a tamer place since it started charging a membership fee. Still, SI remains one of the preeminent message board sites, especially for more serious discussion of tech stocks and widely followed issues. A strictly enforced code of conduct and prohibitive user fees seem to have culled a lot of the penny-stock hype that used to be rampant on this Web site.

Smart Money (www.smartmoney.com). This site, a companion to *Smart Money* magazine, offers investors a wealth of ideas, news, and research. It is loaded with opinions, editorials, analyses, educational features, and other goodies. You might want to check out Smart Money University, a free on-line investment course with quizzes. There's also a useful section ranking discount, online, and full-service brokers. If you're a beginner, it's not a bad site. More experienced investors will probably want to skip it.

Stockmaster (www.stockmaster.com). If you like charts, you'll love Stockmaster. Created by Mark Torrence when he was a student at MIT, Stockmaster was the first site to offer free stock charts on the Internet. Today, the site offers sophisticated but easy-to-read and easy-to-use charts. Beginners and experienced technical analysts alike will love these charts. The site is fast loading and easy to use, but, notwithstanding its excellent charting features, it's rather bare.

The Investment FAQ (www.invest-faq.com). A truly unique site, the Investment FAQ (frequently asked questions) is exactly what its name implies. There are over 200 questions with detailed, article-length answers on just about every conceivable investment topic. From taxes to trading, stock analysis and regulations, stock splits, and lost certificates, the site is a free, virtual how-to book for online investors. Amazingly, the site itself is the part-time endeavor of one overenthusiastic online investor named Christopher Lott. He doesn't write most of the FAQs. Instead, they come from dozens of contributors, some well-known experts, and, mostly, from ordinary online investors. Lott tirelessly edits them.

The Investors Clearing House (www.investoreducation.com). This easy-to-use investor education site is sponsored by the nonprofit Alliance for Investor Education. Here you'll find a few good articles, primers, and quizzes that can help answer investment-related questions.

The official site of the NASD OTC Bulletin Board (www.otcbb.com). Notwithstanding its archaic design, confusing navigation, and content written in indecipherable bureaucratese, this is the best Web site where you can get accurate information about OTCBB-listed securities. If you invest in penny stocks and OTCBB-listed securities, this is a must bookmark site. Reliable and up-to-date, the best features include a daily list of changes affecting OTCBB-listed securities. These include symbol changes, name changes, splits (forward and reverse), new listings, and deletions. Another useful feature on the site is a daily list of the previous trading day's most active OTCBB issues. Many of the stocks on the list are exactly the kind we often warn about in this book. Their sudden price and volume increases are often signatures of deliberate stock manipulations or runaway hype.

The Official Site of the SEC (www.sec.gov). This useful and informative site provides a number of features and materials for online investors. Use it to report suspected securities fraud, read up on the latest SEC enforcement actions, research

SEC filings, or peruse the informative investor education materials. You will also find the original EDGAR database here, but we find that the Free EDGAR site is more user-friendly.

TheStreet.com (www.thestreet.com). If you're dying to get the latest scoop from nouveau stock guru Jim Cramer and a ton of other talented writers, this is the only place to come. TheStreet.com is an excellent Web site for up-to-minute news and well researched editorials and opinion. This is the kind of Web site that makes for great after-hours reading. And, fortunately for you, TheStreet.com is now completely free.

Validea.com (www.validea.com). The name seems to mean "Valid Idea" and that's exactly what this unique and clever Web site seeks to do. The site provides a search engine to what editors, analysts, and other published gurus are saying about different stocks. Then Validea.com goes a step further. By following the results of those ideas, it compiles a track record for each opinion giver and for each stock. This is a great site for sorting out the credibility of those who regularly dispense investment ideas. Don't miss this one.

Wall Street Journal Interactive Edition (www.wsj.com). The Wall Street Journal Interactive Edition is probably the best thing that ever happened to *The Wall Street Journal* print edition. Ever the quintessential financial and stock market news publication, *The Wall Street Journal* endeared itself to thousands of loyal subscribers by allowing them to pay $150 less per year to get the "Journal" online. This is a great site. Its principal attraction is the wealth of original news and in-depth reporting the *Journal* is famous for, much of which you cannot find on any other Web site. You can search for articles from the print *Journal, Barron's,* and the Dow Jones news service. Be sure to check out some of the great "Heard on the Net" columns. If you're going to subscribe to only one pay-for-news site, this one is it.

Yahoo! Finance (quote.yahoo.com). One of the most comprehensive and popular financial destinations, Yahoo! Finance serves up a plethora of features and tools for investors. Since Yahoo! isn't in the business of writing news articles and, in general, manufacturing its own content, it relies on aggregating content and features from a variety of sources, all of which are hungry for exposure on Yahoo!'s highly trafficked sites. The result is the best-of-the-best online financial content providers almost seamlessly integrated into one easy-to use Web site. Message boards, stock games, news, charts, quotes—they're all here.

Zacks (www.zacks.com). Earnings, earnings, earnings. That's what Zacks is all about—and more. Even before the Internet, Zacks was compiling and publishing earnings estimates and consensus for its newsletter subscribers. Today, Zacks offers more earnings information and other raw stock research than most other sites. If you like numbers—lot's of them—in your stock research, this is the place to go.

GLOSSARY

Ve have designed this Glossary to do more than define words. New terms, new meanings for familiar words, new companies, new names for old companies, Web sites, overseas locations for multinationals—these information bites are often written down when discovered and nowhere to be found when needed. Instead of tacking them to a bulletin board or writing between the crossed-out lines of your address book, use these A-to-Z pages for recording new words and their meanings, names/addresses/numbers, or any other information you need quickly. The defined terms are listed alphabetically. List your information bites for each letter in the remaining space.

annual report—A document sent to every shareholder on a yearly basis, according to SEC rules. The report includes discussion of operations and the company's financial status, which is further detailed in the balance sheet and income statement.

---

ask—The price at which a seller is willing to sell shares.

asset—Something owned—by a business, an individual, or an institution—that can be exchanged for something of value.

authorized shares—The number of shares a company will allow to be issued.

balance sheet—A financial statement showing a company's assets, liabilities, and owners' equity as of a certain date, usually the last day of a month.

bear market—An extended period of declining prices, usually driven by pessimists who are convinced that tough economic times are ahead.

bid price—The price at which a buyer is willing to buy shares.

bid–asked spread—The difference between the bid and ask price.

blue-sky laws—State laws governing new stocks. The issuer must provide detailed financial information and register the securities.

book value—Total assets less liabilities and intangible assets.

broker—In the securities industry, someone who works as a go-between for a buyer and a seller. Individuals must be registered with the exchange on which the designated securities are traded. Alternate term: **registered representative.**

bull market—Prolonged time span in which optimism about the future of the economy pushes prices higher.

buy limit order—An instruction to buy a security only at a specified price or lower.

capital expenditures—Uses of capital such as money to buy or improve valuable assets. Usually, long-term investments such as buildings, land, fixtures, machinery, and furniture are designated as capital.

capital gain—The difference between the purchase price and selling price of an asset, but only when the difference is positive.

cash dividend—A periodic (usually quarterly) payment to shareholders from a company's earnings. Dividends are taxable as income to the shareholders.

cash flow—A company's earnings before depreciation and noncash charges, including amortization.

cash flow from operations—The net cash received directly from operating a business. Does not include extraordinary events, like the sale of fixed assets.

churning—Excessive trading in a client's brokerage account, usually to beef up commissions for the broker. Heavy trading is rarely profitable for the investor.

clear—Finalizing a trade by comparing and agreeing on the details, and then delivering stock in exchange for cash.

clear a position—Ending an investor's position in a stock by disposing of both long and short holdings.

convertible preferred stock—Shares of preferred stock that can be converted into a set number of another type of security (typically, common shares) at a preset price.

convertible price—The cost at which a convertible can be exchanged for other shares.

convertible security—Any security that can be converted into a set number of units of another kind of security, at a preset price.

day order—An instruction to buy or sell shares. The order expires at the end of the trading day on which it is issued.

debt/equity ratio—Comparison of shareholder-based assets and amounts owed to creditors. Calculated by dividing long-term debt by shareholder's equity.

distributions—Payments from company's cash flow, including dividends paid to shareholders from corporate earnings.

diversification—A tactic of spreading portfolio holdings among several types or classes of investments (stocks, bonds, and cash), or within an investment class, as a method of minimizing risk.

dividend—A distribution of corporate earnings to shareholders, as determined by the board of directors. Usually paid each quarter, either in cash or in stock.

Dow Jones Industrial Average (DJIA)—The best known and most frequently cited stock market barometer. A calculation of the average weighted price of 30 actively traded (mainly industrial) stocks. Financial firms have been joined in recent years by nonindustrial companies such as software maker Microsoft and retailer Wal-Mart.

downgrade—A change in an analyst's opinion, indicating a lower result in a stock's future performance.

earnings—Net income for a company during a specific time period.

earnings per share (EPS)—Net profit divided by number of shares outstanding.

EDGAR—Electronic Data Gathering and Retrieval system. SEC's archive of company filings.

Efficient Market Hypothesis—The theory that a free market efficiently prices every stock by instantly reacting to news and other dynamics in the marketplace.

exchange—A central marketplace where stocks, commodities, futures, and bonds are traded. The New York Stock Exchange, American Stock Exchange, and National Association of Securities Dealers Quotation System (Nasdaq) are the main U.S. exchanges.

execution—A broker's completion of a trade by buying and/or selling stock.

exempt securities—Stocks and bonds that are exempt from some SEC and Federal Reserve requirements. One of the most common is exemption from registration.

exercise—An action that puts into effect a right to buy or sell that has been made available in a contract, usually relating to options.

exercise price—The price at which stock underlying an option can be bought or sold during a specific time period.

fair market price—The value assigned to an asset exchanged between a buyer and a seller, assuming that the objective of both is to get the best price possible.

financial plan —A company's outline for its financial future and how it will attain the stated goals.

financial objectives—Goals set forth in a financial plan.

float—The number of authorized shares that are available in the open market. Does not include restricted shares.

fully diluted earnings per share—Earnings per common share, calculated by assuming that all instruments that could dilute those earnings—stock options, warrants, preferred stock, and convertible bonds—have been exercised and converted.

Generally Accepted Accounting Principles (GAAP)—Rules governing accepted accounting practices, ranging from broad principles to procedural details.

goodwill—An intangible asset—based on a company's good name, reputation, and exemplary customer and employee relations—that can be expected to add to the firm's earnings or market value.

hedge fund—For U.S. investors, a private investment partnership that usually takes long and short positions and uses derivatives and leverage to invest in many markets. The fund's general partner traditionally makes a substantial personal investment.

hybrid security—A combination of two underlying investments—for example, the price of a particular commodity could dictate the interest rate on a bond. Also called a derivative.

index fund—A mutual fund that mirrors one of a variety of indexes in an attempt to duplicate its performance. For example, an S&P 500 Index fund would include many stocks from the S&P listings.

indexing—Building a portfolio to match an index, in an effort to mirror that index's performance.

initial public offering (IPO)—A company's first public offering of stock.

intangible asset—Something that gives a company an edge in the market, but does not physically exist. Goodwill, trademarks, licenses, and permits are all intangible assets.

interest—The cost of using money at a specific rate during a specific period of time.

interest expense—Money paid toward interest on a loan.

investor—An individual or institution that has a financial interest in a company.

investor relations—The branch of a company that answers investors' questions and provides information about investment opportunities in the company. The goal is to keep the company in a favorable light throughout the investment and capital markets.

letter of comment—A letter from the SEC suggesting changes in, or asking questions about, a company's registration statement.

leverage—Enhancing a return on an investment without increasing the amount of money invested. Buying on margin and buying convertible securities are examples of leverage.

limit order—An order to buy or sell a security at a specific price.

liquid asset—An asset that either is cash or can readily be exchanged for cash. Examples are: bank deposits or U.S. Treasury bills.

management's discussion—Part of a company's annual report to shareholders. Management discusses financial details, as well as other issues such as expectations for the coming year and the state of the company in general.

margin—The money that clients deposit with a broker so that they can borrow money from the brokerage to buy securities. An initial minimum is mandated by the Federal Reserve: The amount deposited must be equal to half of the purchase price of the security, or at least $2,000. Margin is the difference between the loan from the broker and the market value of the stock purchased with that loan.

market capitalization—A company's market value, based on the price of its issued and outstanding shares of stock. Calculated by multiplying the market price of its shares by the number of shares issued and outstanding.

market order—An order to buy or sell securities at the current market price.

mutual fund—A fund that uses money raised from shareholders to invest in stocks, bonds, or a number of other investment instruments. Mutual funds give small investors the opportunity to diversify their portfolios without making a large initial investment.

NASD—The National Association of Securities Dealers operates under the supervision of the U.S. Securities and Exchange Commission. Its mission is to establish and standardize fair trading practices, enforce security trading rules, and provide a disciplinary body to ensure enforcement.

Nasdaq—The National Association of Securities Dealers Automated Quotations system is operated by the National Association of Securities Dealers (NASD). Nasdaq is a computerized system that provides quotes for over-the-counter stocks as well as some stocks listed on the New York Stock Exchange.

net asset value (NAV)—The market value of a mutual fund.

net income—After all expenses have been paid, the amount of money that is left over. Also called net profit or net earnings.

no-load fund—A mutual fund that has no sales cost or commission attached. It is bought directly from the company instead of through a broker.

odd lot—In stock trading, a less-than-100 group of shares offered for sale. Odd lots usually carry higher commissions.

option—The right to buy or sell a security during a specific time period and for a set price. If the option isn't exercised during that time period, it expires and the owner forfeits the investment.

over-the-counter (OTC) market—Stocks that are not listed or traded on an organized exchange.

par value—The par value of common stock is determined by the issuing company and is used for accounting purposes. It has no relevance to the stock's market value.

P/E; P/E ratio—The price-to-earnings ratio, calculated by dividing the price of the stock by its earnings per share. There are two types of P/E ratios: trailing and forward. A trailing P/E is based on last year's earnings. A forward P/E is based on an analyst's forecast for the coming year. For example, if a stock is now trading at $30 per share and earned $1 per share in the previous year, it has a trailing P/E of 30. If that same stock is expected to earn $3 next year, it has a forward P/E of 10.

portfolio—The combined assets of an individual or institution. Holdings can include stocks, bonds, commodities, cash, or real estate.

preferred stock—A class of stock that specifies a dividend rate. It takes precedence over common stock in both dividend disbursements and asset liquidation. Usually, it does not have voting rights.

program trading—Buying and selling based on computer programs that constantly monitor market conditions and will buy and sell when the actual conditions match those that have been programmed. Programs can be written to maximize profit or to direct portfolio accumulation or liquidation.

prospectus—A written proposal for the sale of securities. The proposal details the company's business plan, financial status, history, pending litigation, and officers, and it explains how the proceeds from the offering will be used. A prospectus for a public stock offering must be filed with the SEC. Mutual funds also issue prospectuses.

proxy statement—Information given to shareholders before they vote on company issues. Usually issued before the annual shareholders' meeting, the proxy statement includes information about items that will be voted on—either in person or by proxy. It also contains information about officers and office seekers, including their salary, bonus, and option plan.

public offering—A sale of securities to the general public, according to SEC rules governing sale and registration.

pump 'n' dump—Stock fraud in which the market value of cheaply acquired shares is pumped up by people who acquired them and who subsequently dump them after the public has started buying them and pumping up the price.

pyramid scheme—Fraud that is executed by getting people to buy into a investment. The perpetrators promise astronomical returns and then use funds from later victims to pay off earlier investors.

quotation—The lowest ask and highest bid prices for a security or commodity.

rate of return—For common stock, the annual dividend divided by the purchase price of the shares.

registration statement—A document filed with the SEC and given to prospective buyers of a new issue of stock. The statement outlines the company's plans for use of the sale proceeds, gives a detailed history of the company's finances and operations, and should include any other information that a buyer would need to make an informed decision.

reverse stock split—A company's reduction of the number of its outstanding shares. The remaining shares will have the same market value right after the split as they did preceding it, but each individual share will be worth more. For example, a company had 10,000 shares outstanding at $1 each (a market capitalization of $10,000) and did a 1-for-10 reverse split. The new capitalization would still be valued at $10,000, but there would be only 1,000 shares outstanding, each worth $10.

risk—The likelihood of losing value or not gaining value.

Rule 144—An SEC rule that determines the conditions allowing for the sale of unregistered securities to the public without filing a formal registration.

scalp—Scalping, which is illegal according to SEC rules, occurs when an investment adviser or stock promoter takes a position in a stock, then recommends the stock, and sells it when the price goes up because of his or her recommendation.

SEC—The U.S. Securities and Exchange Commission, established by Congress in 1934 to oversee regulation of securities.

selling short—The sale of stocks that the seller has borrowed from his or her broker, in anticipation of a decline in price.

sell limit order—An order to sell securities at, but not below, a specific price.

shelf registration—A permission that allows companies to file a registration statement up to two years before actually offering the shares into the market. The registration is valid so long as the company files regular financial reports with the SEC. With a shelf registration, firms are poised to take advantage of the best market conditions as they unfold.

spread—For securities, the difference between the bid and ask price.

stock dividend—A corporate dividend paid in stock, not cash. Usually, payment is in shares of the company, but shares in a subsidiary or spin-off may be paid instead.

stockholder's equity—Ownership calculated by taking capital paid in by investors in return for stock, retained earnings, and donated capital, minus all liabilities.

stock split—An increase in the number of shares outstanding without immediately changing the market value. For example, if a company has 10,000 shares outstanding valued at $2 apiece, it has a market value of $20,000. If it splits its stock two-for-one, it will have 20,000 shares outstanding, each worth $1 apiece, and an identical market value of $20,000.

stop-limit order—An order to buy or sell at a designated price (or better), but not until a stop price has been reached. For example, a stop limit order that reads "buy 100 ABC 50 STOP 51 LIMIT" means a buy order won't be entered until the market reaches 50, at which point a limit order for execution at 56 or better is entered.

stop-loss order—Used to protect profits or prevent further losses, a stop-loss order is an order to sell at a specific price below the current market price.

street name—Securities that are held by a broker, rather than the actual investor, are said to be held in street name.

tangible asset—An asset that is physically obtainable, like cash or real estate, with some exceptions—for example, accounts receivable.

taxable income—Income subject to tax after all deductions have been taken.

10-K—An annual report that must be filed by every publicly traded company in the United States, as required by the SEC. Provides shareholders with detailed financial information as well as a summary of the business's operations and future expectations.

thinly traded—Shares that are not traded often and have little volume.

trade—A purchase or sale of a stock, bond, or commodity future contract.

transfer agent—A company-appointed agent who keeps track of who owns a company's stocks and bonds. The agent also issues and cancels certificates.

underwriter—An investment banker who buys a new issue of securities and then sells them into the open market. The profit, or underwriting spread, is the difference between the primary distribution price and the price to the public.

unsecured debt—Debt that is not supported by specific collateral.

waiting period—The time between the filing of a registration statement and the point when securities can be offered for sale.

wash—Gains and losses are equal.

INDEX